Auschwitz and Absolution

Auschwitz and Absolution

The Case of the Commandant and the Confessor

JAMES W. BERNAUER, SJ

Editor

With contributions by

Martin Bernales-Odino

David Biale

Robert P. Burns

Francis X. Clooney, SJ

Firmin DeBrabander

Beth A. Griech-Polelle

Ruth Langer

Marina Berzins McCoy

Walter F. Modrys, SJ

Bruce T. Morrill, SJ

David Neuhaus, SJ

Stanislaw Obirek

Serena Parekh

Christian M. Rutishauser, SJ

Roberto Saldías, SJ

Kenneth Seeskin

Winnifred Fallers Sullivan

ORBIS BOOKS
Maryknoll, New York 10545

Founded in 1970, Orbis Books endeavors to publish works that enlighten the mind, nourish the spirit, and challenge the conscience. The publishing arm of the Maryknoll Fathers and Brothers, Orbis seeks to explore the global dimensions of the Christian faith and mission, to invite dialogue with diverse cultures and religious traditions, and to serve the cause of reconciliation and peace. The books published reflect the views of their authors and do not represent the official position of the Maryknoll Society. To learn more about Maryknoll and Orbis Books, please visit our website at www.orbisbooks.com.

Library of Congress Cataloging-in-Publication Data

Names: Bernauer, James, 1944– editor.
Title: Auschwitz and absolution : the case of the commandant and the confessor / [edited by] James W. Bernauer, SJ.
Other titles: Case of the commandant and the confessor
Description: Maryknoll : Orbis Books, [2024] | Includes bibliographical references and index. | Summary: "An Auschwitz commandant's confession to a Catholic priest poses a critical challenge to Christian notions of forgiveness"— Provided by publisher.
Identifiers: LCCN 2023021891 (print) | LCCN 2023021892 (ebook) | ISBN 9781626985292 (trade paperback) | ISBN 9781608339877 (epub)
Subjects: LCSH: Confession—Catholic Church—History—20th century. | Höss, Rudolf, 1900–1947—Religion. | Lohn, Władysław. | Forgiveness of sin. | Auschwitz (Concentration camp) | World War, 1939–1945— Prisoners and prisons, German. | World War, 1939–1945—Concentration camps—Poland. | Holocaust, Jewish (1939–1945) | National socialism and religion. | Catholic Church—Poland—Clergy.
Classification: LCC BX2263.P7 A97 2024 (print) | LCC BX2263.P7 (ebook) | DDC 262/.1420943862—dc23/eng/20230627
LC record available at https://lccn.loc.gov/2023021891
LC ebook record available at https://lccn.loc.gov/2023021892

In gratitude to the Jews and Christians

who study the Holocaust and strengthen interfaith relations.

Contents

Part One
The Confession of Rudolf Höss

Part Two
Commentaries on the Confession, Sin, Absolution, and Reconciliation

PREFACE

The Holocaust in general and Auschwitz in particular continue to challenge the living with an endless series of issues to confront and people to remember. Regarding Auschwitz there are, of course, such historical questions as to whether the rail lines to the camp should have been bombed or how much did the world's leaders know about what was happening there. Then there are the more contemporary concerns regarding whether resources should be dedicated to its preservation and the purpose of such conservation. UNESCO has declared it a World Heritage site, to be physically protected as a permanent warning for humanity. The interpretive complexity of that warning is a characteristic feature because no particular group has exclusive control of its meaning. Exploration of Auschwitz is scattered: among others there are historians, literary figures, theologians, filmmakers, surviving victims, perpetrators, and journalists who study and comment on the camp and its significance. As Mark Edward Ruff has emphasized, this diversified community of interpreters guarantees a continuing plurality of approaches and the frustrating absence of any easy consensus.[1]

As for the people to remember, there are two striking projects that are motivated by the conviction that a person is only forgotten when his or her name is not remembered. Israel's Holocaust

---

[1]   Mark Edward Ruff, *The Battle for the Catholic Past in Germany 1945–1980* (Cambridge: Cambridge University Press, 2017).

Center, Yad Vashem, has attempted to identify all those Jews who were murdered during the Holocaust and its "Names Project" now includes almost five million individuals. In Europe, the German artist Gunther Demnig founded the "Stolpersteine" (Stumbling stones) project that places brass plates at the last residences of the victims deported by the Nazis. Well over 70,000 of these commemorative plaques have been laid throughout Europe.

While the more than one million victims murdered in Auschwitz are always present in the consciousness of those writing in this volume, the two individuals whom we examine here, were not victims. Indeed one of them was the very manager of Auschwitz, its Commandant Rudolf Höss for whom the Hebrew curse would be most appropriate: "May his name and memory be erased." The other figure was a Polish Jesuit priest, Fr. Władysław Lohn, whose fluent German made him an ideal candidate for the spiritual conversation Höss requested before execution. Their 1947 encounter might have incited a major controversy but, in the midst of all the historic events taking place that year, the conversation between Höss and Lohn rapidly passed into the silent shadows of the past.

Why concentrate on this particular event from that period's complex historical field? To my surprise, several former colleagues advised me not to focus on this meeting. Isn't it too intimate a religious event to publicize? Haven't the churches apologized sufficiently for their conduct? It is certainly the case that both Roman Catholic and Protestant churches have expressed remorse for their contributions to the denigration of the Jewish religion as well as for their support of anti-Semitism.[2] Still it would be a widely

---

[2]   The most comprehensive collection of these statements may be found in Franklin Sherman, ed., *Bridges: Documents of the Christian-Jewish Dialogue. Volume One: The Road to Reconciliation 1945–1985* (New York: Paulist Press, 2011).

shared view that these statements of apology have not penetrated
the religious culture of the churches' subordinate institutions, let
alone the average communities of the faithful. And explicit denial
continues to grow as does general ignorance of the Holocaust. A
very comprehensive poll from a few years ago indicated that 41
percent of Americans and 66 percent of millennials could not say
what Auschwitz was.[3]

An original inspiration for this study was the volume
composed and edited by Simon Wiesenthal: *The Sunflower: On
the Possibilities and Limits of Forgiveness.*[4] The theme of that work
is contained in its subtitle. When a dying Nazi soldier asks for
forgiveness so that he can die in peace, would you give absolution?
The responses from the various contributors vary but that of Father
Theodore Hesburgh, the long-serving president of Notre Dame
University, expressed a very traditional Catholic view: "My whole
instinct is to forgive. Perhaps that is because I am a Catholic priest.
In a sense I am in the forgiving business. I sit in a confessional for
hours and forgive everyone who comes in, confesses, and is sorry."[5]
Would the Commandant of Auschwitz evoke that same instinct
or would his case be far more complicated? The twenty-five years
since the most recent edition of *The Sunflower* have witnessed an
unparalleled effort of reconciliation between Christians and Jews.
Would that development be reflected in the comments by contemporary scholars?

---

[3]   Maggie Astor, "Holocaust Is Fading from Memory, Survey Finds,"
New York Times (April 13, 2018), A15.
[4]   Simon Wiesenthal, *The Sunflower: On the Possibilities and Limits of
Forgiveness,* revised and expanded edition (New York: Schocken Books, 1976).
[5]   Ibid., 169.

INTRODUCTION

What would the Commandant of Auschwitz confess to the Polish priest he has asked to see? How would that priest react to that request and to that confession? This book aims to rescue from oblivion the extraordinary April 1947 encounter between the Nazi Rudolf Höss and Fr. Władysław Lohn, SJ, the Polish Jesuit priest who heard his confession. Höss left a memoir, which he composed shortly before his confession, and it is this life story that enables us to construct what he most likely said to the Jesuit.[1]

For his part, Fr. Lohn revealed almost nothing about his encounter with Höss, likely for two reasons. First, as a Roman Catholic priest, he was bound by the sacrament of penance to honor an absolute prohibition on repeating any confidence received from a penitent in confession. Second, we may assume that no priest, especially a Polish one, would want to be known for absolving a mass murderer of a million victims less than two years after the end of history's worst war.

There are, however, two explicit mentions of Fr. Lohn's encounter with Höss. The first is dated April 12, 1947, and is contained in a customary brief record of Jesuit community activities. Lohn had spoken informally and in confidence to the other members of his Jesuit community during the recreation period after dinner:

---

[1] Rudolf Höss, *Death Dealer: The Memoirs of the SS Kommandant at Auschwitz*, ed. Steven Paskuly (New York: Da Capo Press, 1996).

April 12. At the recreation Fr. Lohn spoke about his mission of reconciliation with God of the executioner in Auschwitz—Hoess, who was judged in Poland for his crimes against millions of convicted people in Auschwitz and who was sentenced to death. Staying in the prison in Wadowice, he asked for a priest to make a confession, since before joining Hitler he had been a Catholic, but later he denied his faith and blindly followed the criminal leader. With the permission of the Metropolitan Curia in Kraków, the superiors appointed Fr. Lohn [to this task], who on Thursday went to Wadowice where Hoess was kept. There, after a few hours of long conversation, Fr. Lohn received Hoess' profession of faith, and heard his confession flowing from a very repentant heart. On the next day he gave him the Viaticum for the way to eternity.[2]

The second mention of the encounter comes eleven years later in a 1958 sermon that Fr. Lohn preached at the first mass of the newly ordained Jesuit Władysław Kubik. This is Fr. Kubik's recollection of that occasion:

During the sermon at the first mass of Władysław Kubik, Father Władysław Lohn said that when Rudolf Hoess was transported to the prison in Wadowice (Wadowice is closest to Auschwitz, where Hoess was to be punished with death), he asked for a German-speaking priest. Then the Archbishop of Krakow, Cardinal Sapiecha asked Father Lohn whether he or another Jesuit would go to

---

[2] Translated by Damian Mazurkiewicz, SJ, Socius and the Director of Archives of Polish Jesuit Archives in Krakow (November 23, 2021). I am grateful to Fr. Mazurkiewicz for locating this document and for his translation. "Viaticum" in the last sentence refers to the Holy Communion given to the dying. Höss was to be executed just four days later.

meet Rudolf Hoess. Father Lohn knew German perfectly well, so he made up his mind immediately. Their conversation lasted over four hours and ended with absolution and Commander Hoess's return to the Roman Catholic Church. The content of their conversation has never been revealed anywhere. The next day, Rudolf Hoess received Holy Communion during which he was moved to tears. Father Lohn said that Rudolf considered his death right and just. He asked the Polish people for forgiveness.

It can be added that Father Lohn met with Hoess as early as 1940. At that time he went to the commandant of the Auschwitz camp, asking for the release of the arrested Jesuits. Unfortunately, he was sent back with complete refusal.[3]

My writer's task in this volume is to recover imaginatively the likely path of priestly reflection that could be expected of Fr. Lohn in scrutinizing his feelings about the encounter with the Commandant of Auschwitz. This scrutiny is the basis of the diary that is presented here as that of Fr. Lohn. In fact, he did not write such a diary but he almost certainly composed it in his mind's recollection of the most memorable pastoral meeting of his priestly career—indeed, of his earthly life. Meanwhile, much is known about Rudolf Höss, the Commandant of Auschwitz, as a result of testimonies against him at his trial and from his memoirs composed in 1946–47.

The Nazi and the Jesuit had only two encounters. In 1940, Lohn slipped into Auschwitz to find several Jesuits who had been

---

3   Fr. Kubik wrote this testimony in Polish in November 2021, and it was translated by Damian Mazurkiewicz to whom I once again express gratitude. Fr. Kubik recalls in his remark an earlier 1940 meeting between Höss and Lohn when Lohn entered Auschwitz to plead unsuccessfully for the release of several Jesuits from his community.

imprisoned there and, when discovered, was brought to Höss, who allowed him to leave, perhaps admiring Lohn's courage. The second encounter came in April 1947 when, at Höss's request, Lohn heard his confession and, giving him communion, accepted him back into the church, which he had left years before in order to join the Nazi party.

By following Hitler, Höss abandoned his father's plans for him to become a priest. Fr. Lohn was a precocious student who entered the Society of Jesus at fifteen years of age. At the end of World War I, he was sent to Rome where he did his doctorate studies at the Gregorian University, and after some years teaching in Krakow, he was invited back to the Gregorian as a professor. Lohn had a distinguished career as an author and professor of theology both in Krakow and Rome. He published dogmatic works on the Trinity, the Incarnation, and Jesus as a teacher. In 1935, he was appointed leader (provincial) of the Jesuits in southern Poland where, as a result of the war's disruptions, he served two terms, or twelve years total.

Discussions about Auschwitz-Birkenau have often involved both material and spiritual issues. Should it have been bombed by the Allies in order to interrupt the mass murder taking place there? After its liberation in January 1945, should it have been totally destroyed or preserved as a memorial to those who died there? That question was decided in 1947 when the Polish Parliament declared the site a "Monument to the Suffering of the Polish Nation and Other Peoples," and in 1979 it was recognized by UNESCO as a "World Heritage Site." Such recognition has not ended controversy: shouldn't Jews be singled out as the most numerous victims of Auschwitz? The most searing dispute arose from the placement of a cross and the establishment of a Catholic convent adjacent to but visible from the camp. The clash of Christian and Jewish paths of memory could not have been more explicit: the cross, a symbol of redemption for the Christian, had no place at the world's largest Jewish cemetery.[4]

Confessions have been a prominent theme in twentieth-century experience and often appear in literature, cinema, and political studies. There was, for example, Albert Camus's *The Fall*, in which the confessor is transformed into a judge-penitent who summons his interlocutor to reveal his own iniquities because he recognizes that every soul harbors a guilt that begs for punishment and pardon. There were films such as *Amadeus, The Seventh Seal, Death and the Maiden*, and Costas-Gavras's *Confession*. This last film, based on the true story of a Czechoslovakian show trial, reminds us of those many trials that Communist regimes staged as demonstrations of their absolute power and personal corruption. In addition, stimulating the interest in trials and confessions was the postwar effort to prosecute those Germans and their allies who were regarded as war criminals. There was a widespread passion for them to confess their crimes because the war's devastation demanded some human accountability. Katharina von Kellenbach's study, *The Mark of Cain: Guilt and Denial in Post-War Lives of Nazi Perpetrators*, shows how inadequately that demand was met. Landsberg in Bavaria was the central prison for criminals incarcerated by the American occupation forces and its military courts handed down 806 death sentences of which 285 were carried out in Landsberg prison itself. It is startling that among those executed there were only "three unambiguous declarations of regret" for their crimes. Kellenbach asserts that one reason for such a small number was the understanding by the chaplains of their religious mission: "Overall, the prison chaplains failed to grasp the peculiar moral challenges of Nazi criminals and understood their primary

---

    [4]   See Carol Rittner and John K. Roth, eds., *Memory Offended: The Auschwitz Convent Controversy* (New York: Praeger, 1991).

task as pastoral counselors to be helping convicts achieve peace of mind rather than recognition of culpability for atrocities."[5]

Some Nazis did seem to reach toward a form of spiritual accountability for their crimes. Albert Speer was among the best known of the Nazi leaders. He served twenty years in prison after his conviction at Nuremberg and later sought the counsel of spiritual mentors, including the Benedictine monk Athanasius in the monastery of Maria Laach. Speer secluded himself in retreats at the monastery once or twice a year and participated fully in the prayerful activities of the monks. Father Athanasius remembered conversations from his ten-year acquaintanceship with Speer: "I don't think I have ever known a man as aware, as Speer was, of his deficiencies."[6]

Another contending with responsibility for crimes was Franz Paul Stangl, the Commandant of the extermination camp Treblinka, who spoke with journalist Gitta Sereny. After seventy hours of prison interviews, the most that Stangl could conclude was a very weak admission of a measured and nuanced guilt. More striking was the incident revealed by his wife who discovered quite late that Treblinka was a death camp and her husband was its manager. She approached Fr. Mario, a priest whom she knew and, under the seal of confession, told him of her discoveries. She reports this as his response, "He gave me such a terrible shock.

---

[5]   Katharina von Kellenbach, *The Mark of Cain: Guilt and Denial in the Post-War Lives of Nazi Perpetrators* (New York: Oxford University Press, 2013), 29.

[6]   Gittta Sereny, *Albert Speer: His Battle with Truth* (New York: Alfred A. Knopf, 1995), 696. Here I will not enter the debate about Speer's sincerity and the claim that his identity as the repentant Nazi was a myth that was successful because it corresponded to a German population's need for exoneration. The large literature on his case manifests sharp disagreement. A very critical treatment of Speer but a comprehensive overview of the issues may be found in the catalog *Albert Speer in the Federal Republic—Dealing with the German Past* (Nuremberg, Germany: Documentation Centre Party Rally Grounds, 2017).

I remember, he brushed his face and then he said, 'We are living through terrible times, my child. Before God and my conscience, if I had been in Paul's place, I would have done the same. I absolve him from all guilt.'[7] This statement surely lacks credibility. How could this Fr. Mario regard himself as the willing Commandant of a death camp? And what would it mean to absolve Stangl from all guilt when he had not confessed anything? Stangl's wife was trying to evade a conclusion that she had come to admit but then retracted, namely, that her husband would have given up his post if she had presented him with an ultimatum that she would leave if he did not. Her personal guilt for not giving that ultimatum was overwhelming, as Sereny found.[8]

Yet another case of a Nazi criminal's confession is that of Arthur Seyss-Inquart, the committed Nazi who served as the Reichskomissar of the Netherlands, whose fate is mentioned in Lohn's diary. A single example of his cruelty: In retaliation for the Dutch bishops' denunciation of the deportation of Jews in July 1942, he ordered that all Jewish converts to Catholicism in the Netherlands be arrested. Among the two hundred converts arrested were St. Edith Stein and her sister Rosa—both of whom died in Auschwitz. Seyss-Inquart was charged with crimes against humanity for his actions and executed at Nuremburg on October 16, 1946. Before he died, he returned to the Catholic faith of his youth, receiving the sacrament of penance and absolution from Fr. Bruno Spitzl, his prison chaplain. Before execution, he admitted his guilt and his acceptance of the death sentence.[9]

As a professional theologian and Jesuit administrator, Lohn had never been assigned to a prison chaplaincy as a priest, even

---

[7]   Gitta Sereny, *Into that Darkness: An Examination of Conscience* (New York: Vintage Books, 1974), 235.

[8]   Ibid., 360–62.

[9]   See Jozeph Michman, "Arthur Seyss-Inquart," *Encyclopedia of the Holocaust,* vol. 4 (New York: Macmillan, 1990) 1344–46.

though he became a priest confessor for one of the most notorious criminals from World War II. His almost total silence on his experience with Höss is in sharp contrast to the many comments of other pastors and priests about their dealings with Nazi criminals. Among the most loquacious was the Canadian minister William Hull who tried to bring Adolf Eichmann back to his earlier evangelical faith, an effort that failed.[10]

Of the thirteen Germans who are mentioned in Kellenbach's *The Mark of Cain*, the Catholic priest Karl Morgenschweis stands out. He served as chaplain in the Landsberg prison from October 1932 until his retirement in August 1957. This is certainly a factor in accounting for his frequent denunciation of the Allied courts as merely "victors' justice" and for his pleas for pardon. Morgenschweis became a public critic of those courts and their depiction of Germans. In a 1966 speech to an assembly of conservative Germans in Munich, he complained, "No matter how deeply we regret what happened, we need not be ashamed. If the French are not ashamed—you know French history with its events, including what happened to Germans—and if the Russians do not need to be ashamed, etcetera, why should we be ashamed? We are not a nation of criminals! And yet today we are treated like that—abroad." He defends both the honor of the German soldier and his own: "We didn't go out to war to appear as criminals, we were filled with ideals called people and fatherland."[11]

In one prominent case, Morgenschweis proclaims the innocence of Waffen-SS General Oswald Pohl who had overseen fostering

---

[10]   William Hull, *Struggle of a Soul* (New York: Doubleday, 1963). Eichmann's lawyer, Servatius, told Hull that Eichmann did not want a spiritual adviser. Curiously though Servatius also said that Eichmann had told him that "if he did have someone, he would prefer a Jesuit priest; he felt that he would understand his position better than anyone else" (ibid., 11).

[11]   Karl Morgenschweis, Nov. 25, 1966, https://docplayer.org/43495942-Karl-morgenschweis-fuer-wahrheit-und-gerechtigkeit.html. Translation mine.

the economic production of the concentration camps, and so, he was in charge of the enslavement of millions. Pohl was among the last convicted Nazis to be executed at Landsberg, in June 1951. He converted to Catholicism under Morgenschweis's direction, who then assisted in the writing and 1950 publication of Pohl's self-exonerating memoir, *Credo: Mein Weg zu Gott*. In his preface to it, Morgenschweis paints Pohl as a worthy Christian disciple and "never mentions the crimes for which Pohl is sentenced to death. He never calls him a perpetrator, and nowhere in his preface does he accuse him of any specific guilt."[12] This is Rudolf Höss's own description of Pohl:

> One side of Pohl was that of a cold, sober calculator, a numbers man who demanded from his subordinates the greatest sense of conscientiousness of duty and work performance. He pursued violations and negligence in an inhumanly hard way and insisted on having his will and his wishes done without question. Woe to him who dared to cross him and his plans. Pohl didn't rest until his adversary was removed or destroyed. The other side of Pohl was one of a great comrade, helpful with those who got into trouble without it being his fault.[13]

Pohl was a willing servant of the Nazi ideology and its inhuman practices.

We have an excellent understanding of the religious vision that Fr. Lohn would have brought to his encounter with Höss. As a priest, he would have considered himself a representative of Jesus's ministry of reconciliation and unconditional forgiveness. The mandate of the Gospels is forgiveness: "If your brother sins, rebuke

---

[12] Björn Krondorfer, *Male Confessions: Intimate Revelations and the Religious Imagination* (Stanford, CA: Stanford University Press, 2010), 116.

[13] Höss, *Death Dealer*, 316.

him; and if he repents, forgive him. And if he wrongs you seven times in one day and returns to you seven times saying 'I am sorry,' you should forgive him" (Lk 17:3–4).[14] "If you forgive others their transgressions, your heavenly Father will forgive you. But if you do not forgive others, neither will your Father forgive your transgressions" (Mt 6:14–15). "When you stand to pray, forgive anyone against whom you have a grievance, so that your heavenly Father may in turn forgive you your transgressions" (Mk 11:25). In relation to the woman caught in adultery Jesus said, "Let the one among you who is without sin be the first to throw a stone at her" (Jn 8:7). As a Jesuit, he was heir to a centuries-long tradition of confessional practice that emphasized a "whole-life confession." This emphasized an explicit linkage of one's moral activities to the full course of one's life, an integration of personal and spiritual developments. My selection of events from Höss's life in his "confession" reflects this "whole-life" approach.[15]

As a Jesuit who annually engages in the practice of the Spiritual Exercises, Lohn would not have been naïve about the human capacity for sin or the hell that awaited the unrepentant. Among the first of the Exercises, Lohn prays in anticipation of his own personal confession this piece of self-knowledge: "I will consider myself as a source of corruption and contagion from which has issued countless sins and evils and the most offensive poison." The punishment in hell for sin is very graphically presented: the bodies of fire, the wailing and howling, the smells of sulphur and filth, and the remorse of conscience.[16] Scenes of hell seem particularly appropriate to the reality Höss helped fabricate and that his

---

[14] All quotations from the Bible use the translation of the New American Bible.

[15] Markus Friedrich, *The Jesuits: A History* (Princeton, NJ: Princeton University Press, 2022), 210–15.

[16] *The Spiritual Exercises of St. Ignatius*, trans. Louis Pohl (Chicago: Chicago University Press, 1951) 30 (#5), 32 (#s 66–69).

victims endured. For example, in 1946 the Protestant critic Martin
Niemöller said this of his experience in a concentration camp: "In
former times, educated people laughed at the idea that there could
be hell and damnation ... but these [images from the sixteenth
century] are child's play compared to the reality.... Hell came to
earth."[17] For her part, Hannah Arendt found the conceptions of
life after death most suitable for describing the camps created by
totalitarian systems: "Hell in the most literal sense was embodied
by those types of camp perfected by the Nazis, in which the whole
of life was thoroughly and systematically organized with a view to
the greatest possible torment."[18]

Reflecting traditional Jesuit devotion to the Sacred Heart
of Jesus, Lohn would have stressed God's unconditional love for
humanity and for sinners especially. Lohn's attachment to the
Shrine of Divine Mercy that honored the revelations Jesus gave to
the Polish nun Sr. Faustina Kowalska would have had him emphasize God's mercy for sinners during his conversation with Höss.
In fact, Lohn published a meditation on the Sacred Heart of Jesus
not long after his encounter with Höss, and it offers a sense of
how he probably encouraged Höss. In it, he wrote, "The compassion of the forgiving Jesus did not cease at the moment when the
spear pierced his heart on the cross. On the contrary, from this
heart poured forth an inexhaustible source of divine mercy. His
merciful absolution: 'I forgive your sins,' priests have repeated
for centuries in the various languages in all corners of the earth,
whenever they say over the inclined head of the penitent: *Ego
te absolve!*"[19] But there is another scene that should be recalled,

[17]   Cited by Kellenbach, *The Mark of Cain*, 98.
[18]   Hannah Arendt, *The Origins of Totalitarianism* (New York: Harcourt
Brace, 1976), 445.
[19]   *Poslaniec Serca Jezusowego VIII* (Krakow, 1950), 245, cited in Manfred
Deselaers, *"And Your Conscience Never Haunted You?" The Life of Rudolf Höss*
(Auschwitz, Germany: Auschwitz-Birkenau State Museum, 2013), 222–23.

one that would also have been known to Fr. Lohn: in a post-Resurrection appearance, Jesus breathed upon the Apostles and said, "Receive the holy Spirit. Whose sins you forgive are forgiven them, and whose sins you retain are retained" (Jn 20:22–23). Whose sins should not be forgiven, should be retained? Should the crimes of Auschwitz be retained?

So how might we assess the confession of Höss? His final statement declares, "In particular, I caused incredible suffering to the Polish people ... I ask for pardon from the Polish nation. In the Polish prison I first experienced what human compassion means. In spite of all that had happened I was shown a human compassion that I never expected and which shamed me profoundly."[20] Striking is the absence of any specific reference to Jews in his expressions of remorse. In fact, he affirms that "as far as my philosophy of life is concerned, I am still a National Socialist." He maintains that the "necessary expansion of the German living space could have been obtained in a peaceful way."[21] He admits that the extermination of the Jews was "wrong, absolutely wrong" because the "cause of anti-Semitism was not served by this act at all, in fact, just the opposite. The Jews have come much closer to their final goal."[22] Such absence of remorse is consistent with his critical remarks about the Jews in Auschwitz. Omitting mention of their gassing, Höss attributes their death rate to a "psychological condition."[23] While he claims that Jews "cling to each other like leeches," he nevertheless accuses them of lacking a "feeling of solidarity." He asserts that many facing death revealed the names of other Jews still in hiding: "Was it personal revenge, or were they jealous because they did not want the others to live on?"[24] Observing the horrible labor of the

---

[20]   Cited by Deselaers, *"And Your Conscience Never Haunted You?"* 224.
[21]   Höss, *Death Dealer,* 182.
[22]   Ibid., 183.
[23]   Ibid., 142–43.
[24]   Ibid., 160.

Sonderkommando stoically removing bodies from the gas chambers, Höss wonders, "The way the Jews lived and died was a puzzle I could not solve."[25]

This absence of remorse for the Jews is ignored in what can only be described as a campaign to celebrate the Commandant's confession and his return to the Catholic faith. Fr. Lohn never joined in that campaign, but it is otherwise widespread. For example, a 2017 video tells of the "amazing story" of Höss in which a priest asserts that Höss is now in heaven and then adds that priests who had refused to hear his confession may be in hell for that refusal.[26] And this remarkable faith echoes in virtual reality, often imaginatively and especially in the sermons that proclaim mercy. A Polish nun described the Commandant's reception of Communion: "And the guard who was present said it was one of the most beautiful moments in his life seeing this 'animal' kneeling, with tears in his eyes, looking like a little boy and receiving Holy Communion, receiving Jesus with his heart," the nun said. "Unimaginable mercy."[27] A distinguished abbot said in a homily that he was citing Lohn as having claimed, "In all my years I have never seen anyone receive Holy Communion with such devotion. I have no doubt that Rudolf Höss is in heaven. I now pray for those priests who refused to give him the supreme gift of God's mercy." Of course, Lohn never said such a thing, and when I wrote to the abbot for the source of his quotation he replied that it had been from his memory of some presentation, possibly on YouTube, and admitted that he could have gotten it wrong and was appalled to think that his story might have been understood as a "misrepresentation of the horror of Auschwitz" when his intention had been "quite the

---

[25] Ibid, 161.

[26] See "Divine Mercy: The Amazing Story of Rudolf Höss," YouTube, May 17, 2017.

[27] https://www.thedivinemercy.org/articles/divine-mercy-and-commandant-auschwitz.

reverse."[28] Apart from invented stories, there is a theological view, though, that denounces as a "new infernalism" any rejection of universal redemption and belief in the continuing possibility of damnation. It is even suggested that motivating this perspective is the desire for a "postmortal annihilation of the perpetrators following on the heels of the historical annihilation of victims."[29]

There is an opposing view. Höss himself recalls an elderly Jewish man passing him on his way into the gas chamber who, by Höss's account, said, "'Germany will pay a bitter penance for the mass murder of the Jews.' His eyes glowed with hatred as he spoke."[30] How might that Jew have regarded the sacramental absolution for the Commandant? Would it warrant the condemnation of Dietrich Bonhoeffer's mocking of "cheap grace"? This means "grace as bargain-basement goods, cut-rate forgiveness, cut-rate comfort, cut-rate sacrament; grace as the church's inexhaustible pantry, from which it is doled out by careless hands without hesitation or limit."[31] The historian Kevin Spicer would agree. At the end of his study of Catholic priests who had supported National Socialism, he emphasizes how most stayed in the priesthood and went on in the postwar period with their regular lives. They were similar to the church leaders who "followed, like the German public in general" and "were eager to put the National Socialist past behind them. All was forgiven for the glory of God."[32] Rudolf Vrba, who escaped Auschwitz in order to warn unaware Jews,

---

[28]   Email of December 9, 2021. I do not wish to identify the abbot by name because a quotation such as he gave easily enters Holocaust denial web sites, a development that would horrify him.

[29]   Kellenbach, *The Mark of Cain*, 96.

[30]   Höss, *Death Dealer*, 159.

[31]   Dietrich Bonhoeffer, *Dietrich Bonhoeffer Works, Volume 4: Discipleship* (Minneapolis: Fortress Press, 2003), 43.

[32]   Kevin Spicer, *Hitler's Priests: Catholic Clergy and National Socialism* (DeKalb: Northern Illinois University Press, 2008), 234.

especially in Hungary, of what awaited them there, felt that he failed in that mission. Vrba entitled his account in a summary of his judgment on the creators of Auschwitz, *I Cannot Forgive*.[33]

Would the absolution of Höss reflect a spirituality of no consequences for sinful conduct? Was it a theology and a sacramental system that did not examine experience from the side of victims, but rather from that of victimizers? How else may we explain Kellenbach's conclusion? "Contemporary Christian teachings privilege forgiveness and reconciliation over moral discernment and judgment. At the risk of overgeneralization, one can say that for many Christians, forgiveness constitutes an ethical imperative that is given precedence over accountability and justice."[34]

This mantra of forgiveness continued in a dramatic form during the July 2016 visit of Pope Francis to Auschwitz-Birkenau, where he silently prayed and then wrote in the guestbook: "Lord, have mercy on your people! Lord, forgiveness for so much cruelty." In writing this, did Pope Francis neglect an insight from an earlier reflection he had published—that there needed to be a distinction between a forgivable sin and an unforgivable corruption? Wasn't Höss's refusal to express remorse for his Jewish victims a clear example of corruption, of his unwillingness or inability to make a sincere confession? As Francis maintained years earlier, corruption emerges from a dying life that cannot face up to the truth.[35]

Attempting to apply a tougher sacrament of penance was the American soldier, veteran of a more recent war, speaking with regard to Catholic practice, who suggested imposing a penance of

---

[33] Rudolf Vrba, *I Cannot Forgive* (London: Sidgwick and Jackson, 1963). This volume was released in the United States as Rudolf Vrba, *I Escaped from Auschwitz* (Fort Lee, NJ: Barricade Books, 2002).

[34] Kellenbach, *The Mark of Cain*, 25.

[35] Jorge Cardinal Bergoglio, "Corruption and Sin," in *The Way of Humility*, trans. Helena Scott (San Francisco, CA: Ignatius Press, 2013), 9–56.

one year for each person a soldier killed, "exclusion from Communion and a diet of bread and water for the prescribed period."[36] This viewpoint might seem irrelevant for Höss, who faced execution within the week after confession, but might it have justified Lohn in retaining from absolution the sin of mass murder, leaving the judgment to God in the afterlife? As early as the second century CE, the Christian writer Tertullian distinguished between sins that were not mortal and could be forgiven by men, and mortal sins that only God could absolve.[37] Is the mandate of ready forgiveness faithful to the mission of Jesus to negate sin and evil, or does it camouflage that evil? Could the sacramental absolution of the confessed sins of Rudolf Höss be considered as among the final atrocities of the Holocaust?

Appreciation for the specific Polish context also leads to a better understanding of how the absolution for Höss might have been regarded by many. In the postwar years, the Communist government had 32,000 trials for war crimes and collaboration, and it sought popular support for punishing war criminals.[38] The Communists marginalized the church, and the church's consequent tendency was to emphasize its own spiritual authority and powers. Any skepticism about the sacrament of penance and its power to cleanse from sin would have been perceived by many as an assault on the church itself, just another step toward an atheistic future.

The postwar situation in Western Europe raises other questions. Was there an escape into religion itself by the general

---

[36] Philip G. Porter, "War & Penance: What the Church Can Offer Soldiers—And the Rest of Us," *Commonweal* 149, no. 1 (2022): 16–20, 18.

[37] Tertullian, *La Pudicité, Sources Chrétiennes* #394 (Paris: Editions du Cerf, 1993), 2, 76, 85.

[38] See Andrew Kornbluth, *The August Trials: The Holocaust and Postwar Justice in Poland* (Cambridge, MA: Harvard University Press, 2021); Gabriel N. Finder and Alexander V. Prusin, *Justice behind the Iron Curtain: Nazis on Trial in Communist Poland* (Toronto: University of Toronto Press, 2018).

population? Were the Nazi figures in that population looking for a more favorable Allied exoneration by returning to their earlier Christian identities? Were some of them sincerely seeking a more merciful Divine judgment in the afterlife for what they had done serving the Nazi state? How do we account for the assistance given to escaping Nazis by some Catholic clergy? Simon Wiesenthal, the well-known investigator of Nazi criminals, believes it was due to a misunderstood notion of love of one's neighbor. And once again, threatened by the growing power of an atheistic communism, clerical perception of the responsibility and guilt of Nazis came to be dominated by the virtue of forgiveness.[39] The conversion of Nazis was regarded as a cornerstone of the postwar re-Christianized Germany and Europe. But how profound was this conversion in Höss and other Nazis? How deep a transformation did Höss experience in returning to the Catholic Church? He had always considered himself a decent and upright person when he was a Nazi and presided over Auschwitz.[40] After his encounter with Lohn, he thought of himself as a good and decent Catholic. Was that a conversion?

Fr. Lohn died less than a year before the Vatican Council II opened in 1962. It is unfortunate that he never had discussions with his fellow theologian Abraham Joshua Heschel, who had left Poland years earlier. Perhaps they would have spoken of Jewish-Christian relations and of Heschel's conversations with Cardinal Augustin Bea, the architect of "Nostra Aetate." Bea and Lohn almost certainly knew one another, because they had spent several years together in Rome. As he indicates in his diary, Lohn probably had heard of the 1960 initiative by the Pontifical Biblical Institute that the Council make a declaration on the Jews. This was the

---

[39]   Gerald Steinacher, *Nazis on the Run: How Hitler's Henchmen Fled Justice* (New York: Oxford University Press, 2011), 148, 285.

[40]   Karin Orth, "Rudolf Höss und die 'Endlösung der Judenfrage," *Werkstatt Geschichte* 18 (1997), 45–57.

first call by a Catholic scholarly body to request such a statement.
Well before the Council, Lohn had shown leadership at the 1946
General Congregation of the Jesuits by being a principal advocate
for the abolition of the order's prohibition against admission into
the Society of Jesus by those of Jewish ancestry.[41] It would not
be wild speculation to believe that his particular concern for the
Jews emerged from his own visit to Auschwitz and from his later
personal encounter with its Commandant. The papal pilgrimages
would come to that same place: John Paul II in 1979, Benedict XV
in 2006, and Francis in 2016, but that would be later.

We do not know if Lohn ever met Karol Wojtyla (later Pope
John Paul II), who was consecrated an auxiliary bishop in 1958 for
the Archdiocese of Krakow, and whose ministry as pope brought
a flourishing of relations between Jews and Catholics. A landmark
of that new relationship was his confession of the church's sin in
regard to the Jewish people and his plea for forgiveness. At the
beginning of the new millennium, he prayed: "God of our fathers,
you chose Abraham and his descendants to bring your name to
the nations: We are deeply saddened by the behavior of those who
in the course of history have caused these children of yours to
suffer, and asking your forgiveness, we wish to commit ourselves
to genuine brotherhood with the people of the covenant." John
Paul II insisted upon a communal, ecclesial dimension in his
plea, and this was so unprecedented that a lengthy justification
from the church's theological commission was required.[42] The
pope's insistence emphasizes the inadequacy of only individual

<hr>

[41] See "Postulatum PP. Kerremans, Mikus, Lohn, Borbely, Arntzen,
Braun: De impedimento ex origine Judaica," *Acta Congregationis Generalis
XXIX (1946).* Jesuit Archives, Rome.

[42] "Service Requesting Pardon" (March 12, 2000), *Origins* 29, no. 40
(March 23, 2000), 648. The justification is in the church's International Theo-
logical Commission document "Memory and Reconciliation: The Church and
Faults of the Past," *Origins* 29, no. 39 (March 16, 2000), 627–44.

confession when dealing with the crimes of anti-Judaism, antisemitism, and the Holocaust. Not only did individual Catholics sin,
but the "Holy Church" bore some responsibility for the failings
of its followers.

It has taken many years for Polish Catholics, and Catholics in
general, to embrace the program of a new relationship between
them and Jews, and that project is still a work in progress. Poland's
situation was particularly sensitive at the end of the Second Vatican
Council: "When Nostra Aetate was adopted, the main 'project' of
the Polish Catholic Church was not about Jews: it was the effort to
defend the Church against the reproach of treason formulated by
the government in reaction to the 1965 Episcopal letter to German
bishops containing the famous declaration '*Przebaczamy i prosimy
o przebaczenie*,' that is, we forgive you and ask for forgiveness." The
Polish Communist regime was not to look away from Catholic
efforts to forgive perpetrators or collaborators of Nazi crimes.[43] Fr.
Lohn well knew the spiritual dilemma in which he had been placed
by history, at the intersection of the conflict between a demand for
justice and the church's insistence on sacramental reconciliation. It
is but one of the dilemmas that this confessional event creates and
that Part One presents. Our commentators will explore the event
and its other challenges in Part Two.

---

[43] Stanislaw Krajewski, "The Reception of 'Nostra Aetate' and Christian
Jewish Relations in Poland," *Kirchliche Zeitgeschichte* 29, no. 2 (2016) 295–96.
For the exchange of letters, see Otto Roegele, ed., *Versöhnung oder Hass? Der
Briefwechsel der Bischöfe Polens und Deutschlands und seine Folgen* (Osnabrück,
Germany: A. Fromm, 1966).

Part One

The Confession of Rudolf Höss

Selections from *Death Dealer: The Memoirs of the SS Kommandant at Auschwitz*[*]

Rudolf Höss, peace be with you. You have requested that a Catholic priest visit you. That he might help you to examine your conscience, hear your confession, forgive you your sins and give absolution?

"May the Lord be in thy heart and on thy lips, so that thou mayest rightly confess all thy sins."

I commanded Auschwitz until 1 December 1943, and estimate that at least 2,500,000 victims were executed and exterminated there by gassing and burning, and at least another half million succumbed to starvation and disease making a total dead of about 3,000,000.[1] Yes, I was hard and strict. As I see it today, often too hard and too strict. Yes, I said many a bad word in anger over the

---

[*] With the exception of the material printed in italics that has been contributed by James Bernauer, all statements in the confession are those of Rudolf Höss. They are excerpted from Rudolf Höss, *Death Dealer: The Memoirs of the SS Kommandant of Auschwitz*, ed. Steven Paskuly, trans. Andrew Pollinger (New York: Da Capo Press, 1996), and printed here with the permission of Prometheus Press. Numbered page references to this edition follow the excerpts.

[1] Höss affidavit, April 16, 1946, in *Trial of the Major War Criminals* (Nuremberg, Germany, 1947), 415.

deplorable conditions, or the carelessness, and said many things which I never should have done. But I was never cruel, nor did I let myself get carried away to the point of mistreating prisoners. A great deal happened in Auschwitz, presumably in my name, on my direction, on my orders, about which I neither knew, nor would have tolerated, nor approved of. However, all this did take place in Auschwitz, and I am responsible for it because according to camp regulations: the camp Kommandant is *fully responsible* for everything that happens in his camp.

I became a different person in Auschwitz because in general I could not rely on my staff. Until then I always saw the good in people, until I was convinced otherwise. My gullibility had often fooled me. However, in Auschwitz, where I saw myself cheated and disappointed at every step of the way by my so-called coworkers, I changed. I became suspicious. Everywhere I saw only deceit and day after day I was disappointed. In every new face I looked immediately for malice or the worst in everyone. Because of this I hurt and snubbed many honest and decent men. I was unable to confide in or trust anyone anymore. The feelings of comradeship which had been a holy concept to me appeared to be a farce. I felt this way because my old comrades so disappointed and deceived me.

I did not want to have anything to do with them socially. I repeatedly put off going to such social events, and I was glad when I could find a suitable excuse for my absence. This behavior of mine was constantly thrown up to me by my comrades. In fact, Glücks himself pointed out several times that in Auschwitz there were no comradely ties between the Kommandant and the officers. I just couldn't do it anymore. I had been disappointed too much. More and more I was withdrawing into myself. I buried myself in my work and became unapproachable and visibly hardened.

My family suffered because of it, particularly my wife, because I was unbearable to live with. I saw only my work, my duty. All human feelings were pushed aside by this. My wife tried repeatedly to tear me away from this isolation. She invited friends from outside the camp to visit us, as well as my comrades from the camp, hoping that this would draw me out and help me to relax. She arranged parties away from the camp even though she disliked the social life as much as I did. Now and then this pulled me out of my self-imposed isolation for a while, but new disappointments quickly drove me back behind my wall of glass.

Even people who hardly knew me felt very sorry when they saw how I behaved. But, I didn't want to change. I became unsociable in certain respects because of the tremendous amount of disappointment I experienced. Often, even when I was with friends I had personally invited I would suddenly become untalkative or even rude. I would have loved to run off and be alone because I suddenly felt that I didn't want to be among other people any longer. That's when I struggled to pull myself together and tried to get rid of the bad mood by drinking. With alcohol I became talkative again and at times funny and even loud.

In general, alcohol put me into a happy mood, and I wished the whole world well. I have never had an argument with anyone when I was drunk. In this mood people were able to coax out of me things which I would have never revealed when I was sober. However, I never drank when I was alone, and I never had a craving for alcohol either. I also never got dead drunk or let myself go too far because I had too much to drink. When I felt I had had enough I quietly disappeared. I was never derelict in my duty because I had too much to drink. No matter how late I came home I arrived for work in the mornings completely refreshed. For disciplinary reasons I also expected my officers to behave the same way at all times because there is nothing more demoralizing for subordinates than when the superior is not there at the start of work because he got drunk the night before. My attitude about this was not very popular.

You say you became a different person in Auschwitz. How do you understand your responsibility for this transformation?

My parents gave me the freedom to do as I wanted because my father had made a vow that I would lead a religious life and become a priest. The way I was raised was entirely affected by this. I was raised in a strong military fashion because of my father. Because of his faith, there was a heavy religious atmosphere in our family. My father was a fanatic Catholic. During our time in Baden-Baden, I seldom saw him because he traveled for months at a time or was busy with other matters. This all changed in Mannheim. My father now took the time every day to give me some attention, whether it was to look over my schoolwork or talk about my future vocation as a priest. I especially liked his stories about his service in East Africa: his descriptions of the battles with the rebellious natives, their culture and work, and their mysterious religious worship. I listened in radiant rapture as he spoke of the blessed and civilizing activities of the missionary society. I resolved that I would become a missionary no matter what, and that I would go into darkest Africa, even venture into the center of the primeval forest. It was especially exciting when one of the old, bearded African fathers who knew my father in East Africa came to visit. I did not budge from the spot so that I would not miss a single word of the conversation. Yes, I even forgot all about my pet horse Hans.

My parents constantly had guests at our house so they seldom went to parties. Our house was the meeting place for the religious from all areas. My father became even more devout as the years passed. As time allowed, he would take me on pilgrimages to the holy places of our country, yes, even to the hermitages in Switzerland and Our Lady of Lourdes in France. He fervently prayed for heaven's blessing so I would become an inspired priest. I myself believed deeply, as much as one can as a child, and I took my religious duties seriously. I prayed with the proper childish reverence and was zealous as an altar boy. I was taught to obey all adults, especially older people, and treat them with respect no matter what the circumstances. Most of all, it was essential to be helpful, and this was my highest duty. It was emphatically pointed out again and again that I carry out the requests and orders of parents, teachers, priests, and all adults, even the servants, and that this principle be respectfully obeyed. I was not permitted to leave anything unfinished. Whatever they said was always right. This type of training is in my flesh and blood.

I can still recall how my father was a determined opponent of the Kaiser's government because he was such a fanatic Catholic. But in spite of his political views, he constantly reminded his friends that the laws of the government were to be obeyed unquestioningly. Even from childhood on up, I was trained in a complete awareness of duty. Attention to duty was greatly respected in my parent's home, so that all orders would be performed exactly and conscientiously. Each person always had certain responsibilities. My father paid special attention to see that I obeyed all his orders and instructions, which were to be carried out painfully. I can still remember a time when he got me out of bed because I left the saddle blanket hanging in the garden instead of in the barn where he told me to hang it to dry out. I had simply forgotten about it. He repeated over and over that from little things which seemed unimportant carelessness generally develops into great tragedy. I did not understand what he meant at the time; only later would I learn through bitter experience to follow those principles.

A warm relationship existed between my parents, full of love, full of respect and mutual understanding. And yet, I never saw them being affectionate to one another. But at the same time, it was very seldom that they exchanged an angry or bad word between them. My two younger sisters were four and six years old. They were around my mother a great deal and loved to cuddle with her, but

I refused any open show of affection, even from my early years on, much to the constant regret of my mother and all of my aunts and relatives. A handshake and a few brief words of thanks were the most that one could expect from me. Although both of my parents cared for me very much, I could never find a way to confide in them. I would never share any problems, either big or small, which occasionally depress young people. Inwardly I struggled with all these things by myself. The only one I confided in was my Hans. He understood me, as far as I was concerned. My two sisters were very attached to me and tried repeatedly to form a good, loving relationship with me. But I never wanted to bother with them. I played with them only when I had to and then annoyed them until they ran crying to mother. I played many pranks on them. In spite of that, they cared deeply for me, and I regret to this day that I could never display a warm feeling for them. They always remained strangers to me.

I respected and admired my parents very much, my father as well as my mother. However, love, the kind of love which I came to know later as a parent, I could not pretend to show for them. Why was this? I cannot explain, and even today I can find no reason.

How and why did you set aside the plan that you become a priest?

The first serious crack in my religious belief happened when I was thirteen years old. On a Saturday morning, during the usual pushing and shoving to be the first one into the gym, I accidentally pushed a classmate down the stairs. Throughout the years, hundreds of students must have sailed down these stairs without any serious injuries. This time he was unlucky; he broke his ankle. I was punished with two hours of detention. I went to confession in the afternoon as I did every week, confessed what I did like a good boy, but I didn't say anything about this incident at home because I didn't want to spoil Sunday for my parents. They would learn about it soon enough during the coming week.

That evening my confessor, who was a good friend of my father, was visiting at our house. The next morning my father scolded me about the pushing incident, and I was punished because I did not report it to him right away. I was devastated, not because of the punishment, but because of this unheard-of breach of confidence by my confessor. Wasn't it always taught that the secrecy of the confessional could not be broken? Even the most serious crimes that a person tells a priest in the holy confessional cannot be reported to the police. And now this priest, whom I trusted so deeply, who was my steady confessor and knew my whole little world of sins by heart, had broken the secrecy of the confessional for such a minor incident. Only he could have told my father.

Neither my father, mother, nor anyone else from our house had been in town that day. Our telephone was out of order, and none of my classmates lived in our neighborhood. No one had visited us except my confessor. For a long, long time, I checked all the details about this over and over because this was such a horrible thing to me. Then and even now I am firmly convinced that this priest had violated the secrecy of the confessional. My faith in the holy profession of the priesthood was smashed and doubts began to stir within me. I never went back to him for confession because I could no longer trust him. I told the priest that I was going to our religious instruction teacher in the church near my school because my father lectured me when he discovered I was no longer going to this priest. My father believed it, but I am convinced that the priest knew the real reason. He tried everything to win me back, but I just couldn't go back to him. In fact, I went even further. I didn't go to confession at all anymore if I could get away with it. After this incident I could no longer trust any priest.

In religious instruction we were told that if a person went to communion without confession, he would be severely punished by God. We were told that someone had done that and had dropped dead at the communion rail. With childish simplicity I begged God to be lenient because I could no longer confess faithfully and to forgive my sins, which I now recited directly to him. So I believed I was free of my sins. Full of doubt, I went trembling to the communion rail in a strange church. And nothing happened! So I, poor little earthworm, believed that God would hear my prayers and agree with what I was doing. The deep, true, childlike faith which so calmly and surely guided my soul until this time was smashed.

In early 1917 our outfit was transferred to the Palestine front in the Holy Land. All the familiar names from religion, from history, and from the legends about the saints came back to me again. And how different it was from the way we had pictured it in our youthful fantasies from descriptions and pictures. At first they used us at the Hejaz railway station, then later at the front lines near Jerusalem.

One morning, as we returned from a long reconnaissance ride on the far side of the Jordan River, we met a line of farmers' carts loaded with moss in the Jordan Valley. We had to check all vehicles and pack animals for guns because the English tried in every way imaginable to deliver guns and ammunition to the Arabs and to other nationalities who wanted to overthrow Turkish rule. We asked the farmers to unload their carts and started to talk to them through an interpreter, who was a young Jewish boy. They explained to us that they were bringing the moss to the monasteries for the pilgrims. This didn't make any sense to us at all.

A short time later I was wounded and taken to a field hospital in a German settlement in Wilhelma, between Jerusalem and Jaffa. The settlers there had emigrated a generation before for religious reasons, from the state of Württemberg in Germany. In the hospital, I learned from these people that there was a very profitable trade in the great quantities of moss brought to Jerusalem. The moss is an Icelandic variety, gray-white netting with red dots.

The pilgrims were told that the moss came from Golgotha, and that the red dots were the blood of Jesus. It was sold for a great deal of money. The settlers openly told us about the profitable business there was from the pilgrims in peacetime when thousands flocked to the holy places. The pilgrims, they said, would buy anything connected with the holy places or with the saints. The large pilgrim monasteries were the best at it. They tried everything to get as much money from the pilgrims as possible. After I got out of the hospital I looked into this in Jerusalem. Because of the war there weren't many pilgrims, but there were many German and Austrian soldiers. Later I saw the same thing going on in Nazareth. I talked about it with my comrades because this trivial traffic in so-called holy objects by the Church disgusted me. Most of my comrades didn't care and said that if the people were so dumb to fall for such a fraud, they would just have to pay for their stupidity. Others just thought of it as a tourist industry which happens at special places. Only a few, as deeply Catholic as I was, condemned these activities of the Church. They too were disgusted by the sick manipulation of the sincere religious feelings of the pilgrims who often sold everything they owned just to see the holy places once in their lives.

For a long time after my discharge from the army I tried to come to terms with what I experienced, and this was probably the reason I later left the Church. I would like to state that the comrades of my outfit were all staunch Catholics from the Black Forest. During that time I never heard any words spoken against the Church.

Even during the war, I had doubts about my vocation to be a priest. The incident with my confessor and the trade in holy relics that I had seen in the Holy Land had destroyed my faith in priests. I also had many doubts about the Church. Little by little I began to reject the profession my father had always praised, but I didn't consider any other profession. I never spoke to anyone about this.

Before my mother died she wrote in her last letter that I should never forget what my father wanted me to be. I struggled with my feelings of rejection toward the priesthood and with my desire to respect my parents' expectations.

What goal replaced the plan to be a priest?

The soldier within me blossomed. Throughout many generations my ancestors on my father's side had been officers. In 1870 my grandfather died as a colonel leading his regiment. My father was a soldier, body and soul, even though his religious fanaticism concealed this passion after he left the army. I wanted to be a soldier and I didn't want to miss this war. My mother, my guardian, and all my relatives wanted me to finish school first. They said that then there would be time to discuss it. Besides, I was supposed to become a priest. I let them talk while I tried everything to get to the front lines. I often hid inside the troop transports and rode with them until I was caught. In spite of my most passionate pleading, the military police brought me back because I was too young.

And your experience as a soldier in war satisfied you?

I had not fired a single shot as I fearfully watched the slowly advancing Indians.[2] I can still picture to this day a tall, broad Indian with a distinct black beard, jumping from a pile of rocks. For a moment I hesitated, the body next to me filling my whole mind, then I pulled myself together even though I was very much shaken. I fired and watched the Indian slump forward during his jump. He didn't move. I really can't say if I aimed correctly. He was my first kill! The spell was broken. Still unsure of myself, I began firing and firing, just as they had taught me in training.

---

[2]   The reference is to the Indians who were fighting on behalf of the British during World War I.

In the hospital at Wilhelma, a young German nurse took care of me. It was at this time that I had my first sexual experience. I had been shot through the knee and also suffered a terrible relapse of malaria which lasted quite long. I needed special care and had to be watched closely, since I caused a great deal of damage during my delirious ravings due to fever. This nurse took care of me so well that my mother couldn't have done better. As time passed I noticed that it wasn't motherly love which caused her to nurse me in such a loving way. I had never been in love with a woman until then. I had heard about sex in discussions with my comrades, and the way soldiers talk is quite explicit, but I didn't have these desires, perhaps because of the lack of opportunity. Also, the hardships and strain of the campaign didn't exactly bring out feelings of love. Her tender caresses, the way she propped me up and held me, confused me at first, because I had always avoided showing affection, but now I was under the magic spell of love and saw her with different eyes. This love for me was a miraculous experience. She led me through all the steps of love-making, including intercourse. I would not have had the courage to do this. This first experience of love, with all its tenderness and affection, became the guideline for the rest of my life. I never again could joke about sex. Sexual intercourse without affection became unthinkable for me. So I was spared from having affairs and from the brothels.

World War I ended. I had matured far beyond my age, both inside and out. The experience of war had put an indelible mark on me. I had torn myself from the security of my parents' home and my horizons had widened. In two and a half years I had seen and experienced a great deal. I met people from all walks of life and had seen their needs and weaknesses. The schoolboy who had run away from home and trembled with fear during his first battle had become a rough, tough soldier. At the age of seventeen I was decorated with the Iron Cross and I was the youngest sergeant in the army.

The Indian soldier may have been your first killing, but later you were accused of a political murder and you were sentenced to prison. What effect did that have on you?

Most importantly, I overheard their [other prisoners] discussions at the windows during the evening. And those conversations gave me insight about the thinking and psychology of this class of criminals. An abyss opens up to me about human aberration—vices and passions.

At the start of my time in prison, one evening I overheard one prisoner in a nearby cell tell another how he robbed a forester's house after making sure that the forester was safely seated in a tavern. During the robbery he killed the maid with an axe, then murdered the wife, who was in her final month of pregnancy. After that he took the four little children, one by one, and smashed each head against the wall until they stopped screaming, because they were crying. He told about this foul deed with such vile and brazen expressions that I would have loved to get at his throat. I could not get to sleep that night. Later on I heard about many more depraved things, but they did not upset me as much as what I had first heard on that day.

The cell block in this respect was a real confessional. I heard many a window discussion in Leipzig during my pretrial custody discussions in which husbands and wives poured out their inner troubles and comforted each other—discussions in which accomplices bitterly accused one another of betrayal, and those which the prosecutor would have been greatly interested in and by which many a dark crime could have been cleared up. At that time I was amazed that through the windows the prisoners so freely and fearlessly told one another often deeply hidden things which were to be kept secret. Was this compulsion to tell one another born of the privation of solitary confinement, or did it stem from the general human desire to tell things to each other?

In my opinion, many of the inmates could have been brought back on the right path if the prison officials would have been more humane than just doing their jobs, particularly the priests of both denominations, who just by censoring the letters, alone were aware of the frame of mind and condition of their flock. But all these officials had become gray and dulled by the constant monotony of the work. They didn't recognize the inner needs of the person who was seriously wrestling to become better. If an inmate really got up his courage to ask his spiritual counselor for advice about his inner conflict, it was at once assumed that he wanted to play the penitent sinner in order to get paroled. There is no doubt that the officials had experiences in which they were fooled by those not worthy of compassion and understanding. If there was the slightest expectation, even the most cynical criminals suddenly became very pious when the time for a parole hearing approached. Countless times, however, I overheard prisoners grumbling among themselves how much they needed help from the administration with their inner problems. Such privation had a much more severe psychological effect on the serious prisoners who really wanted to better themselves than the physical hardships and experiences of being locked up could ever have had.

I wanted to pray, but all I could manage was a sad, fearful mumbling. I had forgotten how to pray; I could no longer find the way to God.

In that state of mind I believed that God didn't want to help me anymore because I had left him. My officially leaving the Church in 1922 tortured me. And yet this was only the result of a condition which existed since the end of the war. Even though it happened gradually, I had already cut the ties to the Church during the last years of the war. I reproached myself bitterly for not having followed the will of my parents, for not becoming a priest.

Nevertheless you continued as a soldier after prison?

Himmler asked me to join the SS in June 1934. This now was to pull me away from our planned path. For a long, long time I struggled trying to make a decision. This was not my usual habit. The temptation to be a soldier again was really strong, much stronger than my wife's doubts about whether this profession would fulfill and satisfy the inner me. She agreed, however, when she saw how very much I felt attracted to becoming a soldier again, even though I would have to deviate from our agreed course. I was confident that we would be able to hold on to our dream, since I was promised quick promotion, and with all the financial advantages connected with it. This goal, the farm as a home, a home for us and our children, remained with us even in the later years. We never deviated from that.

This is when my guilt really begins.

It had become clear to me that I was not suited for this kind of service because in my heart I did not agree with the conditions and the practices of the concentration camp as demanded by Eicke.

My heart was tied to the prisoners because I had suffered their kind of life much too long and had also experienced their needs. Right then I should have gone to Eicke or Himmler and explained that I was not suited for service in the concentration camp because I had too much compassion for the prisoners.

I did not have the courage to do this.

I did not want to reveal myself because I didn't want to admit my sensitivity. I was too stubborn to admit that I had made the wrong decision when I gave up my plans to farm.

I had volunteered to join the active SS. The black uniform had become too precious to me and I didn't want to take it off in this way. If I admitted that I was too soft for the SS, I would have been expelled, or at least been dismissed without ceremony. I did not have the heart for that. So I fought between my inner conviction and my sense of duty. And I struggled with my loyalty oath of the

SS and my allegiance to Hitler. Should I become a deserter? Even today my wife knows nothing of this inner conflict. I have kept it to myself until now.

As an old-time member of the Nazi Party, I believed in the need for the concentration camps. The real *Enemies of the State* had to be put away safely; the asocials and the professional criminals who could not be locked up under the prevailing laws had to lose their freedom in order to protect the people from their destructive behavior.

I was also firmly convinced that only the SS, the guardians of the new state, could perform this job. But I did not agree with Eicke's views about inmates and his method of enraging the basest feelings of hate among the guard troops. I did not agree with his personnel policy of leaving the prisoners with incompetent people; I did not agree with his practice of unsuitable people in their positions. I was *not* in agreement with the length of sentencing depending on someone's whim.

But by staying in the concentration camp, I adopted the views, orders, and decrees which were in force there. I accepted my fate, which I had voluntarily chosen, even though deep inside I quietly hoped to find another kind of duty in the service in the future. At that time, however, this was unthinkable because Eicke said I was very much suited for prison duty.

Even though I became accustomed to all of the occurrences of the concentration camp, I never became insensitive to human suffering. I always saw it and felt it. But I always had to walk away from it because I was not allowed to be soft. I wanted to have the reputation of being hard. I did not want to be thought of as a weak person.

You never became insensitive to human suffering? What about the Jews?

I have always rejected *Der Stürmer,* [Julius] Streicher's anti-Semitic newspaper, because of the disgusting sensationalism calculated to work on man's basest instincts. Then there was also the constant emphasis on sexual matters, which were extremely pornographic. This newspaper did a lot of damage and has never been of any use to serious scientific anti-Semitism. In fact, it has damaged the cause of anti-Semitism by turning people off. It was no wonder after the collapse of Germany I learned that a Jew edited this newspaper and wrote most of the depraved articles.[3]

Such depraved hate campaigns in the manner of *Der Stürmer* did not serve the cause of anti-Semitism. If you wanted to fight the Jews intellectually, you had to use better weapons than this.

I want to emphasize here that I personally never hated the Jews. I considered them to be the enemy of our nation. However, that was precisely the reason to treat them the same way as the other prisoners. I never made a distinction concerning this. Besides, the feeling of hatred is not in me, but I know what hate is, and how it manifests itself. I have seen it and I have felt it.

The original order of 1941 to annihilate all the Jews stated, "All Jews without exception are to be destroyed." It was later changed by Himmler so that those able to work were to be used in the arms factories. This made Auschwitz the assembly point for the Jews to a degree never before known.

The Jews who were imprisoned during the 1930s could still count on the fact that someday they might be released again, which made being in prison psychologically much easier. But for the Jews in Auschwitz, there was no such hope. They knew without exception that they were sentenced to death, and that they would stay alive only as long as they worked. The majority also had no hope or expectation that their sad fate would be changed. They were fatalists. Patiently and apathetically they allowed all the misery,

---

[3]   There is absolutely no evidence to confirm the statement that *Der Stürmer* was edited by a Jew according to Martin Broszat, *Kommandant in Auschwitz: Autobiographische Aufzeichnungen des Rudolf Höss,* ed. Martin Broszat (Stuttgart, Germany: Deutsche Verlags-Anstalt, 1961), 109.

deprivation, and torment to happen to them. The hopelessness of escaping the foreseeable end caused them to become totally withdrawn from what was happening in the camp. This mental breakdown accelerated the physical breakdown. They no longer had the will to live. They had become indifferent to everything and even the slightest physical shock caused them to die. Sooner or later death was certain for them.

From what I observed, I firmly maintain that the death rate of most of the Jews was caused not only by the unaccustomed work, or the inadequate food, or the overcrowded living conditions and all the other unpleasantness and poor conditions of the camp, but mainly and most importantly because of their psychological condition. The death rate of the Jews was not much lower in other places of work in other camps under much more favorable conditions. It is significant that it was always relatively higher than the death rate of other prisoners.

According to Himmler's orders, Auschwitz became the largest human killing center in all of history. When he gave me the order personally in the summer of 1941 to prepare a place for mass killings and then carry it out, I could never have imagined the scale, or what the consequences would be. Of course, this order was something extraordinary, something monstrous. However, the reasoning behind the order of this mass annihilation seemed correct to me. At the time I wasted no thoughts about it. I had received an order; I had to carry it out. I could not allow myself to form an opinion as to whether this mass extermination of the Jews was necessary or not. At the time it was beyond my frame of mind. Since the Führer himself had ordered "The Final Solution of the Jewish Question," there was no second guessing for an old National Socialist, much less an SS officer. "*Führer*, you order. We obey." was not just a phrase or a slogan. It was meant to be taken seriously.

*It was "beyond your frame of mind"? But hadn't your earlier
Christian training taught you that Jews were children of God, fellow
members of the human family?*

As I have said repeatedly, the Jews have a very strong sense of family.
They cling to each other like leeches, but from what I observed,
they lack a feeling of solidarity. In their situation you would assume
that they would protect each other. But no, it was just the opposite.
I heard about, and also experienced, Jews who gave the addresses of
fellow Jews who were in hiding. These Jews in particular came from
Western Europe.

A woman who was already in the gas chamber shouted out the
address of a Jewish family to an SS soldier. One man who, judging
by the way he was dressed and the way he behaved, came from the
best social class, actually gave me a slip of paper on which was a list
of quite a few addresses of Dutch families who were hiding Jews.
I cannot explain what motivated them to reveal this information.
Was it personal revenge, or were they jealous because they did not
want the others to live on?

This incident I witnessed myself: As the bodies were being
pulled out of one of the gas chambers, one member of the
Sonderkommando suddenly stopped and stood for a moment
as if thunderstruck. He then pulled the body along, helping his
comrades. I asked the Kapo what was wrong with him. He found
out that the startled Jew had discovered his wife among the bodies.
I watched him for a while after this without noticing anything
different about him. He just kept dragging his share of bodies.
After a while I again happened on this work party. He was sitting
with the others and eating as if nothing had happened. Was he
really able to hide his feelings so completely, or had he become so
hardened that something like this really didn't bother him?

Where did the Jews of the Sonderkommando get the strength
to perform this horrible job day and night? Did they hope for some

special luck that would save them from the jaws of death? Or had they become too hardened by all the horror, or too weak to commit suicide to escape their existence? I really have watched this closely, but could never get to the bottom of their behavior. The way the Jews lived and died was a puzzle I could not solve.

But how did you solve the puzzle of your own way of life?

I was no longer happy at Auschwitz once the mass annihilation began. I became dissatisfied with myself, my main responsibility, the never-ending work, and the undependability of my coworkers. I was also not happy with my superior's lack of understanding and the fact that he would not even listen to me. Truly, it was not a happy or desirable situation. And yet, everyone in Auschwitz believed the Kommandant really had the good life. Yes, my family had it good in Auschwitz, every wish that my wife or my children had was fulfilled. The children could live free and easy. My wife had her flower paradise. The prisoners tried to give my wife every consideration and tried to do something nice for the children.

Today I deeply regret that I didn't spend more time with my family. I always believed that I had to be constantly on duty. Through this exaggerated sense of duty I always had made my life more difficult than it actually was. My wife often urged me, "Don't always think of your duty, think of your family too."

I am constantly faulted because I did not refuse to carry out the extermination order: the horrible murder of women and children. I have already answered that question in Nuremberg. What would have happened to a squadron commander who would have refused to fly a bombing mission on a city, knowing full well that there were no arms factories, no essential factories, and no military installations; knowing full well that his bombs would kill mostly women and children? He would certainly have been court-martialed. But the Allied interrogators and prosecutors would not accept this comparison. I believe that both situations are comparable.

I am now as I was then, as far as my philosophy of life is concerned. I am still a National Socialist. A person who has believed in an ideology, a philosophy, for almost twenty-five years and who was bound up in it body and soul cannot simply throw it away just because the embodiment of that idea, the National Socialist state and its leaders, acted wrongly. In fact, criminally and through their failure our world collapsed and the entire German people have been plunged into unspeakable misery for decades into the future. I cannot do that.

We have been together for several hours. Should we conclude? Do you have more to confess?

Today I realize that the extermination of the Jews was wrong, absolutely wrong. It was exactly because of this mass extermination that Germany earned itself the hatred of the entire world. The cause of anti-Semitism was not served by this act at all, in fact, just the opposite. The Jews have come much closer to their final goal.

Without realizing it, I became a cog in the wheel of the huge extermination machine of the Third Reich. The machine is smashed, the motor has perished, and I must perish with it. The world demands it.

[After or during the Act of Contrition, Lohn begins the prayers of absolution in a low voice in Latin.] He says, "May Almighty God have mercy on thee, forgive thee thy sins, and bring thee to everlasting life. Amen. May the almighty and merciful Lord grant thee pardon, absolution, and remission of thy sins. May Our Lord Jesus Christ absolve thee, and I by His authority do absolve thee from every bond of excommunication, or interdict (or suspension) as far as I am able and thou art needful. I absolve thee from thy sins in the name of the

Father and of the Son and of the Holy Ghost. May the Passion of Our Lord Jesus Christ, the merits of the Blessed Virgin Mary and of all the Saints, whatever good thou shalt have done or evil endured, be for thee unto the remission of thy sins, the increase of grace, and the reward of everlasting life. Amen."

The Diary of Władysław Lohn, SJ

An Imaginative Composition

James Bernauer, SJ

April 10, 1947

I must admit that fear grips me as I anticipate speaking with Höss. But why? I have met him before when he was master of my life and death, and now he is a powerless prisoner. Even when he was in his uniform, his appearance was not that menacing and the later description of him as resembling a "grocery store clerk" seemed on target. Do I fear that evil is contagious, that he will contaminate me, that my own soul is in jeopardy? Yes, Auschwitz was hell but shouldn't I be accustomed to hell after years of Nazi occupation of Poland? And my religious imagination has been shaped by the tales of Catholic martyrs through the ages. Almost every day at the opening of our community meals we are read stories of torture from the Roman Martyrology. Wasn't St. Stephen, our first martyr, stoned to death? We hear of later victims who were stretched on racks, whipped, starved, their eyes and flesh torn from their bodies. Is Auschwitz worse than the hell of those torments? Does Höss show a more blood-thirsty cruelty than that of the Roman Emperors?

So, I will now meet for a second time the Nazi official who imprisoned my brother Jesuits and who supervised the destruction of so many Jews, Christian Poles, and peoples of other nations. He has asked to speak with a priest, and for a Catholic prisoner facing death that usually means he wants to make a confession. And Höss was a Catholic? I will soon find out what sort of Catholic he was and already I wonder what will be a suitable penance for the Commandant of a death camp? There is no guidance for that from any manual that I studied in theology. But isn't that a distraction? I must keep my focus on the love of Christ for all, even sinners, especially sinners. And that is why this morning I stopped in at the Convent of the Congregation of the Sisters of Our Lady of Mercy where the mystic Sister Faustina Kowalska lived and where she was graced with visions from Jesus and Mary. I asked the Sisters to pray for me and for my meeting with Höss at which I will emphasize the Sacred Heart, love as the center of Christ's life, and, thus, of the Christian's existence. I will assure him that God's love expresses itself in an unlimited mercy for sinners. While remembering that truth throughout my meeting, I must also recall for my own humility messages that are reported to have been spoken to Sister Faustina by Our Lord Himself: "When you approach the confessional, know this, that I Myself am waiting there for you. I am only hidden by the priest, but I Myself act in your soul." "The person of the priest is, for Me, only a screen. Never analyze what sort of a priest I am making use of; open your soul in confession as you would to Me, and I will fill it with my light."[1] I am a mere instrument, only a screen. That will inoculate me against any personal arrogance in thinking that I should judge that man's soul. And that is consolation for me.

Still, I am frightened. Will his confession save him from hell but condemn me to everlasting punishment? What will the people of Poland think when they hear that a priest, a Polish priest nonetheless,

---

[1]   *Divine Mercy in My Soul: Diary of Saint Maria Faustina Kowalska* (Stockbridge, MA: Marian Press, 2020) 569, #602; 610, #1725.

has given absolution to the German manager of mass murder in Auschwitz? Will my family name be forever disgraced?

Was there difficulty in finding a priest for this confession? Many, perhaps most Poles, regard Höss as an animal, a beast not able to receive the sacrament of penance. But doesn't that attitude just imitate the view the Nazis themselves took on their victims whom they saw as *Untermenschen*? Some priests probably excused themselves because they claimed their control of German was inadequate but I have my doubts about such professions of linguistic weakness. Would that I never learned German! Cardinal Sapieha has now asked for a Jesuit and as provincial, I volunteered myself. Why put pressure on another Jesuit to do it, especially if Höss, remembering our encounter in 1940, requested me by name—which it seems he has?

Having spoken them many times, I have long memorized the words of the ordinary penitential ritual, but now I wonder if there will be need of a stronger supplication, the prayer of exorcism. Will I encounter in Höss the disguised presence of Satan himself, who will need to be expelled? This is the heart of the prayer that I will be prepared to recite in an exorcism that the Cardinal has authorized me to perform if I judge it necessary: "Begone, Satan, inventor and master of all deceit, enemy of man's salvation. Give place to Christ in Whom you have found none of your works; give place to the One, Holy, Catholic and Apostolic Church acquired by Christ at the price of His Blood. Stoop beneath the all-powerful Hand of God; tremble and flee when we invoke the Holy and terrible Name of Jesus, this Name which causes hell to tremble, this Name to which the Virtues, Powers and Dominations of heaven are humbly submissive, this Name which the Cherubim and Seraphim praise unceasingly repeating: Holy, Holy, Holy is the Lord, the God of Hosts."

But what am I thinking? Wouldn't the exorcism of Höss simply confirm that he was the plaything of cosmic forces and that he was not responsible for what he had done? "Satan made me do it." But the entire logic of confessional practice rests on the freedom of the penitent. There is no sin if one was not able to choose between good and evil. It is not surprising that the church authorizes exorcisms so rarely and only under strict conditions. Höss's crimes were certainly satanic but need one be possessed by some demon to commit them? Is the lure of potential exorcism by me precisely to deny that? I am not responsible for the sins I commit, the cowardice I manifest. "The devil did it!" Too easy an out, for him and me. Would I be a witness to the unspeakable suffering and murder of his victims or would my exorcism force them to endure a second death, a holocaust without real human agency and responsibility?

Postencounter Diary Entries

Imagined for April–May 1947

So now I have listened to the voice of evil but also of a plea for forgiveness.

I felt queasy when he said that he had been preparing for the priesthood as a young man and that his father was passionate in urging and training him to embrace this vocation. The priesthood! But these plans were undermined when he thought his father's priest friend had revealed a sin he had confessed. I find myself daydreaming about what sort of priest Höss might have become. Arrogant? Overbearing? A master of the clerical style?

Then I feel anxious in thinking that the two roles, priest and Commandant, may have resemblances and provide some explanation for how Höss could feel so comfortable in his position. Both figures stand on pedestals, the holy priest and the elite SS man. Both represent gods, judges of life and death. Both are consecrated to absolute authorities, the living God and Jesus's delegate, the pope, on the one hand, and to providence and its ruling Führer, on the other. And isn't there an eerie parallel in that the ordination of a priest is considered to imprint a permanent character on the soul while certainly the identity of Höss will always remain the Commandant of Auschwitz? Isn't mass murderer as profound an "ontological change" as Catholics believe occurs with priestly ordination?

After World War I, there was an intense search in Germany for a savior figure to redeem the sacrifices of the war, and Höss found that messiah in Adolf Hitler. And for Höss there was an intense kinship between the priest and the soldier, the two figures that competed in his life plans: Both roles are defined by the willingness to take orders.

His father brought him to places of pilgrimage, and Höss mentioned Lourdes in southern France, a site that is so well known to me. But what did he learn or remember from visiting it? For me and for so many others Lourdes embodies the gospel in a pure form, displaying a Christian face that could not be avoided and that brings consolation. The overwhelming presence on the streets and in the basilica is of the disabled; of the handicapped and of the seriously ill; of ever-present hospital gurneys, stretchers, and wheelchairs. My memory is of the daily processions that involved hundreds and, depending on the season, thousands of the infirm and, most movingly, of the blind who carried their candles as they sang hymns to Our Lady, the great comforter. These are the proud citizens of a kingdom of the sick. How could Höss come to embrace its very antithesis, a death camp organized for the murder of the handicapped, the disdain of the unproductive, the declaration of lives unworthy of life?

Höss recalls with gratitude that a nurse showed delicate care for him when he was hospitalized during the World War, even to the point of sharing sinful sexual intimacy with him. But then, not so many years later, this same man heartlessly supervises the so-called euthanasia of children and all the others? Now I seek solace in echoing the well-known cry that Bishop von Galen gave us in his 1941 sermon, when he protested Nazi murder of the sick and handicapped: "O most sacred heart of Jesus, grieved to tears at the blindness and iniquities of men, help us through Thy grace."

I reminded Höss of Christ's forgiveness of the two criminals who were being crucified with him. The Savior's compassion for others continued as he was drawing his last breath. From the cross Jesus forgave the worst of sinners, his own murderers, and so I have merely joined my voice to that of his in forgiving Höss. That was my priestly duty. My priestly duty! Am I just imitating what the Nazis themselves proclaimed, that they were just following orders? Am I claiming to be just following the orders of my Lord? Much as the crusaders claimed as they pillaged and murdered Muslims? Or as inquisitors asserted in sending heretics to the stake? I am deeply troubled at what this confession and absolution is revealing about me.

Another lesson he might have learned at Lourdes was how the young girl Bernadette courageously stood up to skeptical authorities in defense of the visions of Our Lady that she insisted were hers. As has been the case with most of the Nazis, Höss explains and justifies his criminal conduct by claiming he was under the obligation to obey orders. He confesses that obedience was the paramount virtue in his upbringing and its perfect practice was considered the proof of his religious maturing. In listening to him, it struck me that he does reflect the pathology in much of religion, especially its sanctification of submissiveness.

I have always felt uncomfortable with the story of Abraham's willingness to sacrifice Isaac and with some presentations of Jesus's obedience to the Father in the Crucifixion. And let's face it, we Jesuits are not without blame for the mind-set of people such as

Höss. Our founder Ignatius of Loyola's 1553 letter on obedience and the Society's Constitutions forged demonic expressions as a legacy to future history. The letter puts forward an ideal of responding to an order by proceeding "blindly, without inquiry of any kind, to the carrying out of the command, with a kind of passion to obey." The Jesuit Constitutions adopt an infamous image of this passion: "We ought to act on the principle that everyone who lives under obedience should let himself be carried and directed by Divine Providence through the agency of the superior as if he were a lifeless body, which allows itself to be carried to any place and treated in any way."

Rhetorically, Jesuit documents are some of the sources of that cadaver obedience (*Kadavergehorsam*), which became such a prominent idol in the moral pantheon of Nazism. Rudolf Höss wrote that Hitler's important aide Martin Bormann was very impressed with the Jesuits. Bormann's home was adjacent to the Jesuit house of studies in Pullach, outside Munich, and he admired what he saw as the Jesuit capacity for unconditional subordination and regulation. My God, what has our Catholic and Jesuit legacy to civilization actually been? Have we been preaching a spirituality of no consequences? Just obey the commands of our religious leaders and that is the guarantee that we are doing God's will. And does this obedience parallel the forgiveness in confession? Confess our sins and no matter what we have done, absolution will be given.

Still, what choice did I have but to forgive him? Jesus tells Peter that forgiveness must be given seventy times seven, in other words, endlessly (Mt 18:21–22). With the woman caught in adultery, her accusers are challenged by Jesus's invitation for the person without sin to cast the first stone and, of course, none do (Jn 8:1–11). Isn't the Parable of the Prodigal Son one of Jesus's greatest teachings (Lk. 15:11–32)? But am I merely seeking a way out of the uneasiness I feel in giving God's forgiveness to a mass murderer?

And scripture does give us some examples of an unforgiving God. Although I am not sure what precisely they are: sins against the Spirit, the turning away from God, are everlasting sins and cannot be forgiven (Mt 12:31–32; Mk 3:29; Lk 12:10). Abraham does not help the repentant rich man who is in hell while the beggar Lazarus is in paradise (Lk 16:19–31). Of course, was the rich man really contrite, or was he only trying to escape torment?

My experience with Höss has made me question the customary meaning of this parable. The rich man does not repent: he does not regret his indifference to Lazarus. He wants his brothers warned about what will happen to them if they live as he lived. The rich man fails to understand his own sin. In the same way, Höss only cares about his own family and that is not repentance. Far from it. Even in the case of the prodigal son, isn't it an economic plight that moves him to return to his family and not genuine repentance? He has squandered his inheritance and his father rejoices at his return, not his repentance. Does Höss deserve absolution? Are his crimes beyond the very framework of sin, confession, and forgiveness?

I recall from my classes in canon law that there are several sins for which absolution cannot be given by the regular priest but must be sent to higher ecclesiastical authorities. One is the solicitation by a priest of sex during the confession itself. Another is the profaning of a host that had been consecrated as Christ's body and blood. A third is physically assaulting a priest, bishop, or pope.[2] But canon law did not imagine the crime of a millionfold mass murder. In any case, church law puts aside all these restrictions if the penitent is facing death, and that is certainly the case for Höss now.

Dante's *Divine Comedy* seems more relevant as a resource for this case, than does canon law. Murderers deserve the punishments of hell because it was established by the justice of God. There are even different levels of the state of purgatory for those who delay

---

[2] Canons 1387, 1395, 1367, 1370.

their repentance and who need to be purified of their sins before entering God's presence. Even if Höss is sacramentally forgiven by his confession a few days before execution, we can imagine the almost endless period of purging he will need to undergo before heaven. With such vivid images of hell and purgatory the poet is far more nuanced than the church lawyer in paying tribute to justice and human sentiments.

Still, I gave him absolution for the sins he confessed and I gave him communion, and so he is now reintegrated into the community of the Catholic faithful. What else could I have done?

Nothing. Could I have walked out and told Höss to face God on his own? Yes, it is God who forgives but, as a priest, I was ordained to be an instrument of his mercy. But does even God have the right to forgive sins against human beings by a human murderer who does not believe in God?

Perhaps it is evasion on my part, but I am not alone in giving absolution to high-profile Nazi criminals. The Nazi administrator of the Netherlands, Arthur Seyss-Inquart, received the sacrament from Fr. Bruno Spitzl. Seyss-Inquart deported thousands of Jews to death camps, including the philosopher Sr. Edith Stein. Still, I continue to have doubts about how sincere his contrition is. Many ex-Nazis announced a return to Christian belief, but was that merely an appeal to the courts for leniency in sentencing them?

Höss had no chance for that, and certainly there are indications of his change of heart. In his last letter to his wife, he counsels her not to "lose your faith in humanity" and to seek consolation in the Christian faith. He voices his gratitude to the Polish people for the humane way he was treated in prison. He renounces his service to the Nazi ideology, which he now recognizes as "completely wrong." And his final statement is his clearest apology: "My conscience forces me to make the following declaration: in the seclusion of my detainment, I arrived at the bitter knowledge of how enormous my crime against humanity has been. As commander of the Auschwitz extermination camp, I executed part of the horrible human extermination plans of the 'Third Reich'. Thereby I caused the greatest harm against humanity and human solidarity. In particular, I caused the incredible suffering to the Polish people. I am atoning for my responsibility with my life. May God forgive me my actions one day."

So why am I still doubtful of his sincerity? Well, what is one to think when he also writes this to his wife and children: "But what good does all the weighing and balancing do? Was it right or was it wrong? In my opinion all our paths through life are predestined by fate and a wise providence, and are unchangeable." There is no reform of the person reflected in that statement.

The greatest source of my doubt is that he never mentions the murder of the Jews in his declaration. How could this be? He was an important manager of their destruction, and there is no expression of remorse for this. Not to be forgotten is the fact that, even when he was back in Berlin in a new position, he was recalled to Auschwitz to preside over the murder of almost one-half million Hungarian Jews. He was so efficient that this slaughter of the Hungarians was named "Operation Höss"! His conversation with me was very critical of Jews, and he repeated derogatory fantasies about their conduct in the camp. He even claimed that the editor of *Der Stürmer* was a Jew, and there is absolutely no evidence for that. He then goes on to assert that, in the end, that journal did not really serve the cause of anti-Semitism! Was he continuing to embrace that cause? His repentance might be more convincing if he had ever expressed the desire to confess his crimes to a Jew rather than request the presence of a priest.

I am troubled by the thought that Höss's attitude may just be an expression of the Catholic mentality in general. Has Pope Pius XII expressed remorse or, for that matter, has any other church leader? At least Höss has now requested pardon for his crimes against the Polish people, but has the church done even that? Wasn't the pope silent about the suffering of both the Polish and Jewish peoples? Is Höss being held to a higher standard? I do not know, and that uncertainty troubles me. These days, many, perhaps most German bishops are speaking out against the trials of the Nazi criminals, denouncing them as examples of victor's justice. Does their nationalism blind them to the atrocities committed in the name of the German nation? Didn't that blindness also affect the Jesuits who proudly served in the German military and its so-called defense of Christian Europe against the hordes of atheistic communism? I recall the self-critical, chilling lament of the Jesuit chaplain from World War I, Karl Egger, who denounced chaplains in his book *Seele im Sturm* for their inflammatory words in support of the war and who, thus, became henchmen of murderers or, in a phrase I will never forget, "vampires of war."

And it is not just a problem for German bishops. Wasn't our own leader of the international Jesuit society, Wlodimir Ledóchowski, poisoned by a sinful Polish patriotism that identified communism with Jews and that led him to an anti-Semitism? There are rumors that even Pius XI had grown tired of the superior general's constant hostility toward the Jews. In the eyes of many Jesuits, Ledóchowski's anti-Semitism was real, and there is more than a little evidence for it. How account otherwise for his silencing of the French scripture scholar Joseph Bonsirven who spoke with such reverence for the Jewish scriptures?

Yet, I am touched in a very personal way in thinking of Ledóchowski. He appointed me provincial of the southern region of Polish Jesuits. What did he see in me? A willingness to obey no matter what? I have heard it said that Pope Pius XII surrounded himself with Jesuit associates precisely because they could be counted on to obey. This was unlike so many high church dignitaries who had a certain independence. Should I be troubled by the possible meaning of my appointment?

The Catholic poison goes beyond German and Polish hostility to Jews. Isn't it rooted in our very faith? The coming of Christianity is interpreted as rendering Judaism obsolete, and don't Jews continue to incur the wrath of God for not converting? For putting God's beloved Son on the cross and becoming a deicide people? Isn't that why the Jews lost their land and were sent into exile and diaspora? We Catholics were given little reason by our tradition, let alone our bishops, to regard Jews as beloved of God, as worthy of respect and care. And we Catholics have now reaped the whirlwind. When I recall some of the preaching I did on the anti-Jewish passages in the New Testament, it is difficult not to become physically ill. Fortunately, a more fraternal relationship between Jews and Catholics may lie in our future after the war's traumas.

A major source of my hope for this transformation was my experience in attending, in my position as provincial, the 1946 Jesuit General Congregation. The experience and qualities of so many of the Jesuits who participated in this meeting were overwhelming, and I often felt awed. For years I had been reading my fellow theologian Henri de Lubac who had been heroic in his resistance during the Nazi occupation of France and had been outspoken in his criticism of church leaders. At times I wondered how he felt being in the same room with Norbert de Boynes who had publicly insisted that Jesuits owed allegiance to the government of Vichy.

There were two interesting Americans I admired. Vincent McCormick who became rector of the Gregorian University in 1934, just as I left the faculty to assume my position as provincial in Krakow. He expressed his shock at how many Jesuits in Rome were pro-Fascist and he gave me an insight into why Jesuits might have found fascism appealing: revenge. He told me of a conversation in which de Boynes asserted that the French deserved their military defeat and occupation because France had abandoned God and embraced secularism. So, there is a religiously fueled resentment toward the modern world in general! I did find odd, however, McCormick's fear that the religious leadership of the world might pass on to Protestant countries because of the war on Nazi Germany by the United States and Great Britain.[3] Isn't that to forget that there was a Catholic resistance to Nazis throughout Europe and the German Jesuit Provincial Augustin Rösch, whom I was so pleased to meet at the Congregation, had been a leader in the resistance and a forceful opponent of the Nazis? Somehow, he had survived imprisonment and was released at the end of the war.

I also spoke with the moral theologian John Ford, who so courageously denounced, during the war itself, the indiscriminate bombing campaign of Britain and the United States as immoral in its violation of just war principles. At the Congregation, I joined with several other Jesuit representatives to eviscerate the scandalous 1593 prohibition against admission to the Jesuits of those with Jewish ancestry. Even Rudolf Mikus, from Slovenia, joined with us in making the proposal. The war had obviously changed his attitude because I remember he was reported to have said in 1939 that Jews should be removed from public life, although he qualified that call by adding that the expulsion must be done with justice, whatever that could possibly mean.

There were other less distinguished delegates to the Congregation and even one American who seemed to advocate a tightening of the entrance restrictions on those with some Jewish ancestry. He was from New York, where the greatest concentration of Jews

---

[3]   These remarks attributed to Vincent McCormick are based on McCormick's unpublished diary. An article by James Hennesey gives an overview of the diary: "American Jesuit in Wartime Rome: The Diary of Vincent McCormick, S.J., 1942–1945," *Mid-America: An Historical Review* 56 (1974), 32–55.

currently live! Still, the strong majority of Jesuits voted to abrogate the 1593 prohibition against Jews, almost four hundred years after its adoption. And we elected a new superior general, Jean-Baptiste Janssens, who had participated in a Belgian resistance group that had rescued Jewish children.[4] A corner has perhaps been turned, and we will see what the future brings.

Imagined for December 1960

So many years have passed, and yet those two days in April 1947, have lodged themselves at the eternal center of my soul—its thoughts, dreams, memories, and prayers.

I have been a theologian at the Catholic Church's most prestigious university, the provincial superior of hundreds of Polish Jesuits, and the director of our Jesuit publishing house. Many would think that good fortune had long shined on me and mine was a very distinguished career. How wrong the judgments of our peers are. My life of seventy years has been defined by two days in April and a conversation with Rudolf Höss. There was a before and there was an after. Most who crossed paths with him would die quickly, unlike me, who has carried his gaze within me, the ever-present gaze of a murderer.

Only on the rarest of occasions have I shared my memory of that encounter and, for me, its ordeal. And this sharing has been almost exclusively with Jesuits from whom I expected compassion and, for the most part, I received it. On the day after bringing communion to Höss, I told the informal group of Jesuits who gathered after dinner in my community of the experience in meeting Höss and of the mission of reconciliation that was mine. They seemed sympathetic but also concerned about how I and Jesuits

---

[4]   On June 24, 1975, Fr. Jean-Baptiste Janssens was declared a "Righteous among the Nations" by Yad Vashem, Israel's Holocaust memorial center.

in general might be perceived if my deed became widely known. Have we given a gift to Communist propaganda? The Communists are holding criminals to account while we Catholics are conferring sacramental absolution. How ironic!

Only once did I recall my experience with Höss in the presence of a large audience made up primarily of laypeople. And that was at the first Mass of the just ordained young Jesuit Wladyslaw Kubik in 1958. Even then, although it was already eleven years later, I merely alluded to the encounter with Höss as an example of how demanding the priest's vocation of reconciliation could become. Some in the congregation may not have even understood whose confession I was referring to. The two years since then have made my attitude more fragile. Part of that growth (or is it regression?) is certainly nearing the death that is coming my way. I want to stand before my Lord and Judge and say that I did more than merely obey church regulations: that I came to conclusions of my own in this collision with evil and pardon seeking.

And perhaps my hope is part of the aspiration for a new post-Holocaust relationship between Jews and Christians. But the situation is certainly looking better, and I am especially proud that the Jesuits at the Pontifical Biblical Institute in Rome were the first academic body to propose a new declaration on the Jewish people and against anti-Semitism to the Preparatory Commission for the upcoming Vatican Council II.

Part Two

Commentaries on the Confession, Sin, Absolution, and Reconciliation

1

Complicit

Winnifred Fallers Sullivan*

The chaplain is, almost by definition, a compromised figure. Serving two masters, the church and the state, the chaplain offers pastoral care to an individual person at the uneasy conjunction of the religious and the secular, whether it is in prison, in the military, in the hospital, or in countless other governmental and quasi-governmental settings. Perhaps in end-of-life situations, the Roman Catholic chaplain is iconically so. Thought to have exclusive power to administer the indispensable "last rites," countless narratives of the dying include a hurried last-minute search for a priest. But the chaplain for an execution acts not just for the person who is about to die. He is there for all of us, church and state, doing the work of forgiveness.[1] The work of the chaplain both reveals and attempts to bridge the gaps in a tidy secular world, always at risk to his own soul, and ours, complicit as he is in the arrangements that define

---

* I am grateful to Hillel Gray, Sarah Imhoff, and Heather Miller Rubens for reading and commenting on earlier drafts of this essay.

[1] For a comparative perspective on some of the issues, see Arzoo Osanloo, *Forgiveness Work: Mercy, Law, and Victims' Rights in Iran* (Princeton, NJ: Princeton University Press, 2020).

his role. Chaplains are witness to the brutal unfinished business of the modern separation of church and state. An individual chaplain speaks for both—and by implication endorses or normalizes their larger projects—each of which is deeply problematic.

Rudolf Höss, Commandant at the Auschwitz death camp for three and a half years, was tried after the war by a Polish tribunal specially created to try Nazi war criminals.[2] Höss testified at length about the hundreds of thousands of deaths for which he was responsible, was convicted, and was condemned to death by hanging.[3] He called no witnesses. His defense was that he had simply obeyed orders. Before his execution, Höss requested to meet with a Catholic priest, a particular Catholic priest, Władysław Lohn, a Polish Jesuit, one of the surviving members of his community, almost half of whom had been put to death in the camp. (Höss and Lohn had met when Lohn went to the camp to protest the imprisonment of his Jesuit brothers.) Höss confessed to Lohn and received communion the morning before he was executed on the very grounds of Auschwitz where he had presided over so much killing. This event is celebrated in preaching and in popular piety as evidence of the extent of God's mercy.

These facts are well known and well documented. Bernauer has in this volume explored through a fictional rendering of Lohn's memory of the experience the profound religious and moral questions raised by this encounter. Here, I want to "step back" from

---

[2] For further information about the Polish tribunal, see Mark A. Drumbl, "Stepping Beyond Nuremberg's Halo: The Legacy of the Supreme National Tribunal of Poland," *Journal of International Criminal Justice* 13 (2015), 903–32; Alexander V. Prusin, "Poland's Nuremberg: The Seven Court Cases of the Supreme National Tribunal, 1946–1948," 24, no. 1 (Spring 2010), *Holocaust and Genocide Studies*, 1–25.

[3] During his imprisonment Höss wrote a lengthy subsequently published memoir: Rudolf Höss, *Commandant of Auschwitz: The Autobiography of Rudolf Höss*, trans. Constantin FitzGibbon (London: Phoenix Press, 1959).

these two individuals and consider the legal context in which their meeting occurred. What was the particular configuration of the modern separation of church and state that framed their encounter? And in what way does its retelling only underline the worst of the tragic banality of the individualism of modern law and of modern Christian theology? Is there a parallel between the incapacities of the still deeply flawed instruments of international criminal law to encompass mass atrocities and the incapacity of the church to address collective/structural sin, its own as well as those of the larger society? Does the scandal of the celebration of Höss's confession in popular Catholic accounts only further dramatize our inability to acknowledge the ongoing toll of social crimes? I cannot address all these questions, but I will briefly expand on their significance. Höss supervised the murder of a million or more people. He said he was just following orders. To condemn him, even to execute him, is arguably to misrepresent the nature of the crime and who was responsible, and to deflect our own complicity in such atrocities. To absolve him compounds the misdirection.

Nazi war criminals have been tried since the end of the war both by specially constituted international courts and by domestic courts. The tribunal in which Höss and forty-eight other defendants were prosecuted was the Supreme National Tribunal of Poland, a special court that operated from 1946 to 1948 under the authority of the 1943 Moscow Declaration signed by Franklin Roosevelt, Winston Churchill, and Josef Stalin. The Moscow Declaration provided that Germans accused of atrocities would be tried under national law in the countries in which those atrocities were committed. The Polish tribunal derived its authority as well from Polish law, both new and old. It was administered by the Soviet-backed new Communist government of Poland, which, using the same laws, persecuted political opponents of the new government. Yet, responding in part to their exclusion by the "Great Powers" from the Nuremberg tribunal, the Polish tribunal's trials were also designed, in addition to punishing the defendants, to showcase Polish legal professionalism and communicate the extent of Polish suffering at the hands of the Nazis. It served punitive, expressive, and pedagogical purposes.

International criminal law scholar Mark Drumbl notes that the Polish tribunal has not received the scholarly attention it deserves, particularly for its legal innovation, well before the trials in Nuremberg, in defining crimes against humanity, genocide in particular, and the effort it made to articulate the relatively new crime of membership in a criminal enterprise.[4] But he also notes that the shortcomings of those trials, as with all subsequent such trials, remain the continued use of a model of individual responsibility borrowed from ordinary criminal law. Drumbl presses us to consider the possibility of defining and punishing collective crimes.[5] Punishing the individual offender in cases of mass atrocity using ordinary criminal law seems to place the bigger picture of collective responsibility in such cases beyond the reach of the law. We can see this in the recent prosecutions in the United States of White police officers for the killing of Black people. As Drumbl says,

---

[4]   Drumbl explains the lack of scholarly attention to the Polish tribunal: "The marginalization of the Tribunal in international legal circles traces to several factors: the influence of the Anglosphere in international criminal law, the anaemic distribution of Tribunal judgments, linguistic barriers, the Cold War divide and unresolved historiographical debates over collaboration and resistance in occupied Poland. The hagiography of Nuremberg as a situs of postwar justice, moreover, colonizes any conversation about the Tribunal." Drumbl, "Stepping Beyond Nuremberg's Halo," 905.

[5]   Mark Drumbl, "Collective Violence and Individual Punishment: The Criminality of Mass Atrocity," *Northwestern University Law Review* 99 (2005): 539–610.

[W]hereas ordinary crime tends to be deviant in the times and places it is committed, the extraordinary acts of individual criminality that collectively lead to mass atrocity are not so deviant. In fact, these acts of individual criminality may support a social norm even though they transgress *ajus cogens* norm. Although this deep complicity cascade does not diminish the brutality or exculpate the aggressor, it does problematize concepts such as bystander innocence, collective responsibility, victim reintegration, reconciliation, recidivism, and the moral legitimacy of pronouncements of wrongdoing by international tribunals when the international community itself is perceived as having failed to prevent the wrongdoing.[6]

Individualized justice, Drumbl says, whether prosecuted in national courts or international courts, focuses on what is seen to be aberrant behavior, thereby providing cover for collective responsibility for violence that is tolerated or even condoned by the majority. And individual forgiveness, whether in the Catholic mode or the Protestant mode, likewise conceals the society-wide sin, such as the enormity of US structural racism. J. Kameron Carter explains this cover-up in an article commenting on the public forgiveness by the younger brother of a Black man murdered by a police officer:

[W]hat I am dealing with here is the American racial structure, not individuals. I'm dealing with why, within the religion of whiteness, whiteness needs black forgiveness to maintain itself. Black forgiveness is part of the ritual work of absolving or extending salvation to America. It is part of the work of re-cohering or saving whiteness in

---

6 Ibid., 549–50.

a moment of crisis. Should such black forgiveness be withheld, whiteness or the American religious project would face a potential collapse. It might suffer a "white out," a possible end of the world or an end of *its* world.

But could the end of the world, a white out, be an alternative understanding of forgiveness, perhaps even an alternative religious orientation? Can there be a forgiveness that does not absolve guilt but brings the antiblack world to an end? Could there be a poetics of forgiveness that pressures forgiveness as we know it? Could there be a forgiveness that ends forgiveness, a forgiveness at the end of the world? Let's hope so.[7]

What of the chaplain? Do the seemingly insoluble legal and political challenges to the prosecution of mass atrocities affect the chaplain's work? The right of a prisoner to meet with a religious representative is enshrined in international law. It is one of those curious moments when secular law acknowledges its incompleteness—perhaps also the enormity of what it is about to do—wishing to share the responsibility. Lohn's role and opportunity was thus defined by the Geneva Convention. As today, chaplains could not object to the legality or morality of the process or of the sentence. The chaplain acts on behalf of the state, as well as the church, a state that kills.[8]

To Google Höss and Lohn is to discover that their encounter has become the stuff of popular piety.[9] Höss's conversion is celebrated

---

[7]   J. Kameron Carter, "How a Courtroom Ritual of Forgiveness Absolves White America," *Religion News Service*, October 24, 2019. Pope Francis's efforts to apologize for the brutality and cultural genocide of residential schooling in Canada might be the beginning of such an effort.

[8]   The ambiguity of the chaplain's role is powerfully represented in literature, as, for example, in Herman Melville's *Billy Budd*.

[9]   For example, John Burger, "The Tragic Yet Hopeful Story of the Commandant of Auschwitz," https://aleteia.org/2023/01/26/the-tragic-yet-hopeful-story-of-the-commandant-of-auschwitz/.

as a strange and disturbing trophy, scrubbing clean the wide responsibility and complicity in Nazi crimes and the persistence of Catholic anti-Semitism and supersessionism, echoing Lohn's own anxieties, as expressed by Bernauer.

It would be deeply misguided not to see ourselves in the ambiguities of Lohn's work, as we must also in the work of killing, now and then.

2

"Führer, You Order. We Obey"

A Historian's Approach

BETH A. GRIECH-POLELLE

As a young undergraduate history major, I can still remember one of my professors, Dr. John Lukacs, explaining to the students in class that history is the search for Truth with a capital T, while the law is concerned with finding Justice. I found the idea of searching for Truth appealing to my idealistic, youthful self. Although I was not quite sure how Truth and Justice might be different in their outcomes, I was intrigued by the nobility of the pursuit of "what really happened." When re-reading some of the final thoughts of Rudolf Höss, my mind immediately drifted back to these undergraduate days and questions and what approach a historian could take when looking at the Commandant's remembrances.

Several years after university, I was standing on the grounds of Auschwitz-Birkenau concentration camp, traveling with a group of professors who teach about the Holocaust. As we stood near the former Commandant's house, we could see the gallows from which Höss was hanged on April 16, 1947. In the summer heat, surrounded by the remnants of destruction and unimaginable suffering, I remember feeling that perhaps Justice had been served at those gallows. But, to this day, historians and other scholars must confront the awful reality that Rudolf Höss was an ordinary man, not a cartoonish cut-out figure, and I am reminded of Holocaust historian Christopher R. Browning's injunction regarding the study of Nazi perpetrators, "I must recognize that in the same situation, I could have been either a killer or an evader—both were human—if I want to understand and explain the behavior of both as best I can. This recognition does indeed mean an attempt to empathize. What I do not accept, however, are the old clichés that to explain is to excuse, to understand is to forgive. Explaining is not excusing; understanding is not forgiving."[1] Browning elaborates further that if one seeks to study perpetrators of crimes, one must acknowledge, no matter how distasteful, that perpetrators are humans too. If one is to go beyond "one dimensional caricature,"[2] then one must attempt to capture as much of the complexity of the human responses as possible. This is vitally important for all students of history; otherwise, we lose the richness of what it means to be human, and we put our study further away from the Truth of what happened. Part of the search for the Truth of what really happened involves corroboration: do we, as historians, have other documents, testimonials, and artifacts that can support the assertions made by those whom we are studying?

Focusing more narrowly on Höss's statements, we can see that we are dealing with a man riddled with contradictions. He is imprisoned and knows that he is facing a death sentence, so he must come to grips with his own decisions and actions. From his final declaration of April 12, 1947, Höss states that his time in prison has allowed him to reflect on the enormity of the crimes

---

[1]   Christopher R. Browning, *Ordinary Men: Reserve Police Battalion 101 and the Final Solution in Poland* (New York: Harper Perennial, 1998), xx.

[2]   Ibid.

he has been responsible for, while simultaneously he indulges in ignoring the specific Nazi extermination project of the Jewish population. Notice his wording: he neither mentions the word *Jew* nor does he emphasize how singularly focused the Nazi regime was on eradicating as many Jews as possible. Instead, Höss speaks more broadly of the "Polish nation" or the "Polish people" and the harm he has brought to them.[3]

If one delves deeper into the former Commandant's thoughts, we are forced to confront the complexities of Höss's personality. Raised in what he referred to as a "fanatically Catholic household," Rudolf was told that he was to become a Catholic priest. Instead, the young man finds that he prefers to be a soldier and eventually abandons his father's plan for him.

Throughout his reminiscences, one can also see that Höss attempts to explain his devotion to authority. From a young age onward, he was taught not to question adults; he stresses, "It was emphatically pointed out again and again that I carry out the requests and orders of parents, teachers, priests, and all adults, even the servants, and that this principle be respectfully obeyed."[4] Clearly, Höss was seeking to establish his ingrained habit of obeying any and all orders, implying that this would be a lifelong trait.

In these types of excerpts, we can find some insight into how he was able to carry on in his position as Commandant of Auschwitz. He points out that his father, although not a supporter of the Kaiser, still insisted on obedience to all earthly authority. So, in reality, Höss could argue that while he did not fully endorse the aims of the Nazi regime, he was still beholden to obey. For many of

---

[3]   Rudolf Höss, Final Declaration, found in Manfred Deselears, *"And Your Conscience Never Haunted You?" The Life of Rudolf Höss* (Auschwitz, Germany: Auschwitz-Birkenau State Museum, 2013), 224.

[4]   Rudolf Höss, *Death Dealer: The Memoirs of the SS Kommandant of Auschwitz*, ed. Steven Paskuly, trans. Andrew Pollinger (New York: Da Capo Press, 1996), 49–51.

us, this explanation leaves a feeling of dissatisfaction as it smacks of the all-too-easy position adopted by so many Germans on trial after the war: they were only following orders and therefore should not be held accountable for their actions.

Höss does dive deeper though. He notes that his guilt began in 1934 when he, at Himmler's request, joined the SS. Why does Höss feel guilt already in 1934? He elaborates by explaining that, although he agreed with the Nazi regime about the need to have concentration camps, he was not a supporter of the ways in which Theodore Eicke ran the camp system. Having been a prisoner himself in the 1920s, he claims that he understood the psychological needs of prisoners stating, "Even though I became accustomed to all of the occurrences of the concentration camp, I never became insensitive to human suffering. I always saw it and felt it. But I always had to walk away from it because I was not allowed to be soft. I wanted to have the reputation of being hard. I did not want to be thought of as a weak person."[5]

While Höss might not have wanted to be seen as "weak," his staff at Auschwitz understood that he disliked that his office was originally located near an improvised gas chamber. He could not tolerate the screaming of the dying victims, so Auschwitz staff had two motorcycles revving their engines during the gassings to drown out the screams.[6]

Höss also wanted to be seen as a man of action, even though he is remembered as a passive victim, simply following orders, as when he states, "But by staying in the concentration camp, I adopted the views, orders, and decrees which were in force there. I accepted my fate, which I had voluntarily chosen."[7] This implies that Höss was merely there at the camp, but, in reality, his position of authority

---

[5]   Ibid., 96.

[6]   Beth A. Griech-Polelle, *Antisemitism and the Holocaust: Language, Rhetoric and the Traditions of Hatred* (London: Bloomsbury Press, 2017), 67.

[7]   Höss, *Death Dealer*, 96.

and his desire to excel led him to find solutions to "problems," such
as being exposed to the screams of the victims. His solution was the
"improvement" of a little red cottage on the grounds of Birkenau,
off in a corner, far removed from his office, sealed, converted into
two gas chambers, and able to kill up to eight hundred people at
one time.[8] Höss was not done with making "improvements" at
Auschwitz, either. By the spring and summer of 1942, he had a
little white house called Bunker 2, fitted with a new gas chamber
that could kill twelve hundred people at one time. Throughout this
time period, thousands of Slovakian Jews lost their lives in both the
red cottage and the white house.

It was clear to Höss by 1942 that if Auschwitz-Birkenau
was going to be a truly industrialized killing center, then further
"improvements" had to be made. By March 1943, the first crema-
torium was opened at Birkenau. Rooms that had once served as
mortuaries were transformed into undressing rooms and a gas
chamber. An elevator was installed that carried corpses out of the
gas chambers up to the ovens. By the summer of 1943, further
gas chambers and crematoria had been completed. With these
"improvements," Höss made it possible to murder 120,000 people
per month.[9]

Höss claimed that, as a former inmate in a prison, he was not
suited to work at a concentration camp: "Right then I should have
gone to Eicke or Himmler and explained that I was not suited for
service in the concentration camp because I had too much compassion for the prisoners."[10] But how much compassion did he, in fact,
have for those destined to die in Auschwitz? How did he feel about
the position of Jews? Here again, he first falls back on "obeying
orders" stating, "The original order of 1941 to annihilate all the Jews

---

stated, 'All Jews without exception are to be destroyed.'"[11] Orders and obedience are a top priority and a reason to carry out murders to Höss. He also feels compelled to say that he had nothing personal against the Jews, yet in the same paragraph contradicts himself by placing Jews into a category of existential threat to Germans: "I want to emphasize here that I personally never hated the Jews. I considered them to be the enemy of our nation."[12]

Höss addresses the specific "Jewish" experience of Auschwitz-Birkenau in various ways. Part of his reflections depict Jews as an amorphous mass, they are all "fatalists" who accept their inevitable death with apathy and patience. He sees them as a giant, indistinct group unable to adjust to the physical and psychological deprivations of the camp, thus blaming the victims for their inability to survive, even stating, "they allowed all the misery, deprivation, and torment to happen to them."[13] Yet there are times when Höss decides to focus on individual Jews in the camp. In one recollection, the Commandant describes watching a Jewish Sonderkommando's reaction to seeing his dead wife's body among the corpses. Höss watched the man, claiming that he could not see anything different about the man's behavior, noting, "After a while I again happened on this work party. He was sitting with the others and eating as if nothing had happened. Was he really able to hide his feeling so completely, or had he become so hardened that something like this really didn't bother him?"[14]

Historians do not have many testimonies from the Sonderkommandos, especially since most of them were systematically killed after a few months of work, only to be replaced by new recruits. We do, however, have the testimony of one survivor, Shlomo Venezia. Venezia was part of a Jewish-Italian community deported

---

[11]   Ibid., 142.
[12]   Ibid.
[13]   Ibid., 142–43.
[14]   Ibid., 160–61.

from Thessaloniki, Greece, to Auschwitz in April 1944. He was selected to work in the Sonderkommando, where he performed the gruesome assignment for eight months. Venezia was in his early twenties; he had already lost his mother and two younger sisters at the initial selections of the camp. He described his first experiences in the Sonderkommando: "Until this point I'd more or less forbidden myself to think about everything that was happening; we had to do what we were ordered to do, like robots, without thinking. But on seeing the body burning I thought the dead were perhaps luckier than the living; they were no longer forced to endure this hell on earth, to see the cruelty of men."[15] As historians, we have insight into Venezia's feelings and can try to use this eyewitness testimony to compare with the Commandant's interpretation of inmates' emotions.

In Höss's memoirs, he continues to accuse Jews of representing an existential threat to Germans. Despite his assertions regarding his extreme sensitivity, he ruthlessly admits that he gave no thought to the orders to annihilate as many Jews as possible. We know that he worked diligently to "improve" the ability to murder hundreds of thousands of victims, particularly Jewish victims. He also continued to reassert his unwavering belief in National Socialist ideology. Could he have resigned and left Auschwitz-Birkenau behind? He states, "I did not have the courage to do this…. The black uniform [of the SS] had become too precious to me and I didn't want to take it off in this way … I did not have the heart for that."[16] What Höss did have the heart for, unfortunately, was turning Auschwitz-Birkenau into the largest industrialized killing facility in human history. As historians, we will never know

---

[15] Shlomo Venezia with Beatrice Prasquier, *Inside the Gas Chambers: Eight Months in the Sonderkommando of Auschwitz* (Cambridge: Polity Press, 2009), 84.

[16] Höss, *Death Dealer*, 96.

what is truly in a person's heart, so finding the Truth in the testimony in a condemned man might be questionable. But it is our duty to investigate such testimony to underscore what human beings can be capable of under extreme circumstances. Understanding is not forgiving.

3

Extraordinary Situations Demand Extraordinary Action

CHRISTIAN M. RUTISHAUSER, SJ

Ethics teaches people to act appropriately and according to the situation in their everyday lives. Ethics formulates general rules. But life also knows extreme situations. For these, extraordinary speech and action are needed. Such a situation is always unique, as is the response to it. General instructions cannot be given. Jesuit Fr. Władysław Lohn was led into such an extraordinary situation, because the Shoah was an extreme situation. The request for confession from a repentant Nazi ideologue and mass murderer like Rudolf Höss challenges an incomparable act. In what sense are the three conditions—repentance, confession, and reparation—according to which a confessional absolution can be granted, applicable here? Or are entirely different categories of reflection needed to act appropriately?

Lohn is aware of the extraordinary situation and struggles with the doctrine of confession as well as with his priestly obligation. Under no circumstances does he want to be guided by instinctive forces at such a decisive moment. He refuses to stylize the Nazi and the Germans as beasts of evil, as much as he can understand this reaction among the victims, Poles as well as Jews. To do so would be to remain entrenched in a racial logic that only inverts the doctrine of the Aryan superman and obscures responsibility and guilt through mythico-religious explanations. Lohn examines Höss's repentance as best he can and finally gives him absolution. But it is significant that he then struggled throughout his life with whether this act was right. The absolution does not bring forgetfulness, the memory remains. Even more, his life would be divided into a time before and a time after the encounter with the mass murderer.

Moreover, it seems important to Lohn that he did not act only in obedience to the church. As high as the virtue of obedience is held in the Jesuit order, he does not allow himself to blindly obey without weighing the consequences. Lohn is aware of how faith in authority and unreflective obedience not only corroded the power of resistance against injustice but how precisely the Nazi extermination machine functioned because its actors invoked the fulfillment of duty, authority, and obedience. And even if forgiveness of guilt and sin is something positive for the confessor, Lohn considers that an absolution given to Höss cannot remain unchallenged by the victims of the Nazis.

As a Jesuit myself, I want to work through the institution of confession to understand the situation Father Lohn was in. Höss was not asking him for a vicarious apology, which the latter was supposed to give as a Pole, as a Catholic, or as a representative of the Jews and other victims, although Lohn is Polish. If Höss were to have asked a Pole or a Jew for forgiveness, this would have been childish and impertinent because, on the one hand, he would be demanding something superhuman from the victim like a child, and, on the other hand, he would be instrumentalizing his victim once again for his own purpose. The situation was also fundamentally different from requested apologies of the kind that have become inflationary in postmodern society. The confession of a mass murderer has nothing to do with asking for empty phrases, nor is it a hollow ritual. Ultimately, Höss's request for a confession was existential and he turned to God. In doing so, he acknowledged that he had not only incurred human guilt but had sinned before humanity and God.

The fact that a priest could forgive sins in the name of God was questionable or even offensive. But confession with absolution is a social form of forgiveness of sins that has grown in history and to which Lohn was committed. It is derived from Jesus's repeated commissioning of his disciples to forgive sins. "Then Peter came to him and asked, 'Lord, how many times must I forgive my brother when he sins against me?' As many as seven times? Jesus said to him, I do not say to you, up to seven times, but up to seventy times seven times" (Mt 18:21f). This strong request, however, does not speak for an absolution for a mass murderer, because Jesus gives an instruction for everyday life.

It seems more important to me that Jesus himself forgave in an extreme situation. He himself became a victim of torture, suffered scorn, scourging, and crucifixion. He himself was killed as a young man and a Jew. But on the cross he asks, "Forgive them, for they know not what they do" (Lk 23:34). And to the repentant criminal who is executed at his side—whatever his guilt—he promises, "This very day you will be in paradise" (Lk 23:43). And what touches me again and again, what is most amazing is that the Risen One appears to his disciples on Easter morning without any rebuke, even though they would have abandoned him, not helped him, fled, or betrayed him. Although himself a victim of torture and murder, no reproach—but also no word of forgiveness—comes from his mouth. Rather, the Risen Lord enters their midst and says, "Peace be with you! Do not be afraid!" (Lk 24:35). He asks Peter, who has explicitly denied him, "Do you love me more than these?" (Jn 21:15), implicitly giving him a chance to make amends. According to John's Gospel, the one raised from the dead even breathes on his own and says, "Receive the Holy Spirit! To those whose sins you remit, they are remitted; to those whose sins you retain, they are retained" (Jn 20:22f). The Gospels thus testify to a will to make possible a new beginning even after extreme guilt. The innocent victim speaks. Resurrection is new creation. Based on these words, does an absolution for a mass murderer perhaps suggest that a priest forgives not only in the name of God but in the name of Jesus, the victim of torture? And is not an absolution to the perpetrator at the same time an invitation for the victims to approach victim Jesus?

But the Risen Lord also says that the disciples can refuse forgiveness. Shouldn't a priest make use of this very reading of the text? Given that forgiveness as well as reconciliation are processes that take time, would this not be more appropriate in the case of Höss? Just as general rules break down at a negative extreme situation, so in any case general instructions for action cannot be derived from a positive extraordinary situation as described in the New Testament.

If one takes seriously the psychological dynamics of victim and perpetrator, but also the religious institution of confession, one cannot help but ask whether Höss really repents. He sees the error of racial ideology and repents for the guilt of mass murder. But does this not remain too general if he does not refer specifically to the extermination of the Jews, of individual suffering? Does Höss show genuine remorse or is he only concerned with grabbing his own salvation? Is insight and repentance even possible in such a short time after the end of the war or is it only about the fear of death, the fear of a divine judgment? And if it were? In addition, the question of reparation must be asked. What would have to be demanded? Is the execution and death penalty Höss faces sufficient?

Is forgiveness possible without falling into "cheap grace," which is an insult to the victims and a new injury to the survivors? Or are there sins against the Holy Spirit, as it says in the New Testament (Mt 12:31f), which cannot be forgiven? If the Holy Spirit is understood as a creative spirit who gives life, then the Shoah represents an anticreation, a radical annihilation, which could well fall under this category.

It is not only confession that places Höss's inquiry into guilt and forgiveness within a metaphysical horizon. Höss asks for confession in the face of his own death. The death sentence on him has been passed. An execution is an extraordinary act in a constitutional state. If one assumes that the judgment on life and death is ultimately reserved for God, then a human court with the death penalty also places itself, as it were, in God's place. The death sentence of a recognized, state court is the counterinstitution to the confession of the church. They stand opposite each other. How must condemnation and absolution be related? Is it perhaps good to keep them in a dialectic? Precisely because the state demands death, must the church take the position of forgiveness? In any case, not only confessional absolution must be problematized, but also the execution of a mass murderer must be critically questioned. Hannah Arendt had done this regarding Adolf Eichmann but met with much resistance.

But let us stay with the death penalty: can it be seen as an act of reparation? Höss cannot give more than his life. But in view of all the suffering he has brought upon people, and in view of the lives he has destroyed, even this calculation does not seem to add up. The death penalty does bring psychological relief to a society, and the evil seems to have been eliminated from the world. But justice is not restored. And what would the situation be like if Höss had been sentenced to life imprisonment? Imprisonment is a form of reparation and keeps open the possibility of returning to society.

Life imprisonment is a response with normal categories to an extreme situation. Confessional absolution probably should have been given only after many years, if at all. Here, too, the interaction of state and church institutions would be needed. And yet the situation remains unsatisfactory.

There is no solution on the human level. Asymmetry abides. The asymmetry remains, especially since suffering is so individual that only the victim himself can forgive. Human substitution is not possible, as Emmanuel Levinas rightly points out. For the victim, one can only demand justice. As a person of the twenty-first century, I wish therefore Lohn had come to act accordingly, and he would have refrained from giving absolution. However, as a Jesuit priest who knows about the existential distress of people, I'm grateful that the metaphysical institution of the confession exists. I must speak out in favor of an absolution, because the suffering of one person less—even if it is the mental suffering of a mass murderer and Nazi war criminal—is a better world. The victims may forgive if God has mercy. "Or is your eye evil because I am good?" (Mt 20:15).

4

What Does It Mean for a
Christian to Forgive?

FIRMIN DeBRABANDER

The case of Rudolf Höss presents Christians with an excruciating
dilemma. When the Polish Jesuit Fr. Lohn absolved Höss for his
sins as the Commandant of Auschwitz, did he perform a magnani-
mous act of Christian charity and demonstrate the marvelous
breadth of God's love, which can encompass even a monster
like Höss? Or, in forgiving the Auschwitz Commandant after a
summary confession and half-hearted (at best) statement of regret,
did Lohn add insult to injury and heap one more offense on top of
the Holocaust?

Höss's statement of confession is quite hollow and misguided.
He is self-absorbed and self-pitying; he would rather talk of his
depression and disillusionment working at Auschwitz (really—
who cares?) instead of the thousands he sent marching to the gas
chamber. Detailing his religious upbringing and ultimate departure
from the faith, Höss underscores the importance of the obedience
engrained in him from an early age. In so doing, he effectively
diminishes his personal culpability for his crimes—he was just

following orders, as even the Catholic Church had taught him to do. Worst of all, he fails to disavow his anti-Semitism. Explaining his regret for his role at the camps, he observes that the camps did not even serve their purpose but backfired: the Jewish people are stronger than ever, or soon to be.

What has Fr. Lohn wrought in the confessional? Should he have bothered with Rudolf Höss? Is Höss a lost cause—his soul so contaminated, so steeped in delusion, and mired in prejudice that it is beyond repair? Has Lohn misunderstood his mission, offering succor to this heinous, irredeemable criminal, while insulting the millions who suffered from the Holocaust?

In defense of Lohn, there is abundant evidence in the Gospel that Christians are not to discriminate against whom they forgive and for what crimes. Yet, we must not read these passages naively. If someone offends us seven times in a day, the Gospel of Luke reports, and asks our forgiveness each time, we must comply—each time. On its face, this seems like a demand for blanket absolution. But we should ask ourselves, what would real mercy look like under these circumstances? What would God's love look like—love that truly reaches the sinner and transforms him? It would not involve impulsive, immediate, unquestioning, and unchallenging forgiveness. If someone offends me seven times in a day, my forgiveness should be different each time; it should be harder to earn, and near the end, almost impossible. Sometimes you must withhold forgiveness—at least immediately—if you would compel your offender to reflect and repent.

I think of my experience as a parent tasked with disciplining my children: if I were to impulsively forgive my son over and over for seven offenses in a row, I would be forgoing my parental obligations—people would say I'm mad. I might say that stricter discipline for each mounting offense is itself an act of forgiveness. It is a testament to the fact that I still love my son that I am open to him—I believe in him and am committed to his ability to change. My responses and demands may be hardly recognizable as forgiveness toward the end, however. Anything less would be a sign of surrender, a sign that I have given up on my errant child.

We must be willing and open to forgive, Luke tells us, but that will look very different in different cases, at different extremes; it will never be simple, nor should it be easy. In any case, the command is that we may not foreclose the possibility of redemption for anyone, ever—that judgment is not for us to make but God's alone. We may never give up on another person; as far as we are concerned, no one is ever a lost cause.

Critics may object to the absolution of Höss on the grounds that he is complicit in evil. His actions cannot, must not, be forgiven. Höss must be damned—he deserves no other fate. *Evil* is a morally problematic notion, however. It evokes what is beyond redemption, and, when applied to individuals, renders them inhuman. This is not helpful in the context of Höss. It is not helpful to suggest that the Holocaust was perpetrated by monsters lacking a conscience. We must insist and remind everyone that the genocide was perpetrated by human beings, moral agents, individuals with responsibility and freedom—and constantly invoke them as such. If we conclude these are acts of evil, we will feel less obliged to understand them and their perpetrators. We may determine they are of another universe altogether—not the universe of comprehensible human behavior. They are utterly alien.

Unfortunately, we cannot accept that the Holocaust was alien. If we would avoid a blood-soaked repeat, we must understand how human beings perpetrated this. We must affirm their responsibility and complicity. We must underscore their agency—they could have said no at any time but did not.

In this regard, Lohn was right to offer Höss confession, because the sacrament of confession individualizes, and it humanizes. It reminds the penitent that he has power, that he is culpable for his actions—he is more than a cog in a machine, or hijacked by an alien force. Confession calls attention to your own sins and shortcomings, which you own as an individual; it calls attention to the role you play in seeing them through, acceding to them, facilitating them, letting them fester, balloon, and grow. And confession calls attention to your duty and power to correct them. Anyone can climb out of a hole, no matter how deep. We must believe this. Why? Because the alternative is intolerable—the alternative is to consign sinners to the misery of their sin, let them wallow in it, and in so doing, wreak more destruction, spread more hate and harm. For the sake of us all, the Gospel insists that no one is beyond redemption. No one is ever so far gone that we should give up and cease reaching out.

Our ability to reach out, our power to forgive is limited, however. How could it be otherwise? We must recognize this, too, when we make judgment on Lohn. I cannot accept that he had the power to absolve, contrary to what Catholic doctrine indicates or suggests. No one can peer so deeply into the soul of a sinner to determine when or if he or she is truly, honestly repentant— or even that he or she is on the right path, making earnest steps. No one can ever know another's hidden aspirations and intentions, whether the person is finally cleansed of prejudice and delusion. That is for God to know. Lohn could not say that Höss was purified or set straight. That is for God to determine. If Höss sincerely wished redemption and transformation, the best his confessor could do is provide intercession and ask God to open his heart.

In a similar way, the penitent ought not to have thought he or she was saved merely through the act of confession, that his or her fate was somehow secure. Sins were uttered to a human ear, processed by a human mind riven with prejudices and limitations of its own. This means his or her confessor's judgment was similarly limited. We should presume that we never know if we are forgiven by God and must continually strive for God's love.

Dietrich Bonhoeffer, who abhors the "cheap grace" doled out by the church on promises of God's boundless love to all, irrespective of their commitment and conversion, reminds us that discipleship and discipline are indelibly linked. To be a disciple of Christ, to be a proper Christian, demands discipline that is never complete. Bonhoeffer quotes Faust in this regard, who "says at the end of his life of seeking knowledge, 'I see that we can know nothing.'" In this lifetime, we are ever in pursuit, never arrived, and certainly never sure of it. We are never sure of our redemption; we are never sure that our confession is satisfactory to God. And "those who want to use this grace [of confession, for example] to excuse themselves from discipleship are deceiving themselves."[1] Confession is a beginning not an end. It should announce and affirm a commitment to ongoing discipline not that it is somehow reaching completion.

I propose that we understand the Gospel prescriptions for forgiveness as an order to retain a spirit of forgiveness, a perennial openness to those who ask it of us. We who forgive are burdened, too; the forgiveness must suit the crime, if you will. It must befit the perpetrators, what they have done—how often, apparently, and for how long—and properly set them on the path to recovery. Forgiveness is an opportunity for self-discipline that we extend to another. It is one step—a perhaps small step—in the larger project of redemption, or discipleship, as Bonhoeffer puts it. We should not expect that a base soul like that of Höss is "cured" by brief visits with Lohn. Höss has a lifetime to correct. He does not have a lifetime to do so. Discipleship, as I understand Bonhoeffer, is a lifetime vocation.

---

[1]   Dietrich Bonhoeffer, "Discipleship," in *The Bonhoeffer Reader*, ed. Clifford J. Green and Michael P. Delonge (Minneapolis: Fortress Press, 2013), 466.

I submit that what Fr. Lohn has wrought is humble. This is not to diminish it in any way, but rather just a reminder that there is only so much he could do with a case like Rudolf Höss. In a way, it's fitting that we do not know what he told Höss in the confessional; otherwise, we would always measure it, analyze it, determine it insufficient or unfair. Confession, as I have tried to argue, is ever incomplete. Focusing on Lohn's words—as on Höss's statement—we might cling to a naïve understanding that forgiveness is transparent, clear cut, or definitive, when in fact it is always provisional and complex, full of nuances we never wholly grasp.

We forgive as a way to ask for God's conversion and grace. It is an invitation, a hand we reach out to a sinner. This expression of openness and humility may prod the same in sinners, so that grace can find a perch in their souls, and break through the layers of lies and excuses they tell themselves—that all sinners tell themselves. Höss was well practiced in similar self-deception. He had decades of practice, and his mounting crimes required ever stronger, more convincing excuses. In ways we cannot detect, perhaps God's grace had penetrated the thick rind of Höss's hardened soul, in meager fashion. In either case, Lohn was justified in reaching out a hand, compelled by his own discipleship, on display for all the faithful.

5

A Critique of Auricular Confession

MARTÍN BERNALES-ODINO

AND ROBERTO SALDÍAS, SJ

The confession of Rudolf Höss before his execution is a fundamental challenge to the Catholic penitential rite. It raises the question of the potentiality of auricular confession concerning someone confessing the creation of a place like Auschwitz. In what follows, we address this challenge in two steps. We characterize Auschwitz's violence as an infernal place and then differentiate the auricular mechanism from the effects promised by the penitential rite and the truth that justifies it. This way of analyzing the issue allows us to conclude that the auricular confession is a mechanism impotent concerning the one who confesses the creation of an infernal space.

Auschwitz

The Auschwitz extermination camp was a singular, collective human creation. It was a place of cruel and unholy creativity, perfected organization to produce a methodical and industrialized extermination of physical life, and a desacralizing of bodies, deaths, burials, and weeping. However, Auschwitz did not only exterminate the physical lives of the murdered. Those chosen to survive endured what Primo Levi called a spiritual shipwreck.[1] Auschwitz produced an inverted metanoia that was the effect of a bewildering penitential ritual that had precise forms of entrances—a humiliating train ride and a surprise arrival at the final station—a veiled baptism that removed the name under which one lived and died and replaced it with a tattooed number, pieces of music played daily, and rites of permanence. Such rites required one to stop hoping; distrust reason; break social ties; forget the value of being human; experience hunger, fear, and permanent catastrophe; and above all, obey to succumb. The inverted metanoia of Auschwitz undermined what could enable resistance and buried what each subject would call human. The penitential ritual that produced this metanoia also created a collectivity of the prisoners and those conducting the penitential rite. Like Dante's description of hell, they all inhabited a place that was destined to create suffering and utilized human energies without affording any hope.[2] We call Auschwitz an infernal place precisely because it cancels hope, produces endless suffering and the radical conversion of its inhabitants. We owe to the work, creativity, and leadership of Rudolf Höss much of the invention and management of this infernal place.

Violence

Any attempt to discursively understand Auschwitz seems fated to recognize its own impotence: words created by free people are not fully capable of capturing what happened there. The violence of

---

[1]   Primo Levi, "If This Is a Man" [1947], in *The Complete Works of Primo Levi*, vol. 1, ed. Ann Goldstein (New York: Liveright, 2015), 194.

[2]   Hannah Arendt was one of the first to use the millenarian image of hell to think about Auschwitz. See Hannah Arendt, *The Origins of Totalitarianism* (New York: Harcourt Brace, 1951, 1979), 438; Hannah Arendt, «L'image de l'enfer» (original text from 1946), in *Auschwitz et Jérusalem* (Paris: Deux-temps, 1993), 152.

Auschwitz seems bound to remain outside our language and, therefore, at the gates of any coherent discourse. If so, Auschwitz shares
the fate of all violence because every discursive effort to apprehend
violence seems impotent and makes it turn away from the effort to
comprehend violence.[3] Despite this impotence, we have not ceased
to undertake these efforts, which follow an impulse that seems
irrepressible. Seemingly, those who write about Auschwitz and
violence make an effort that is as impotent as it is vital, an attempt
that can be profoundly creative. Is it not the attempt to sing the
anger (*mênis*) of Achilles that gives birth to poetry?[4] Is not violence
the background on which the historical categories of philosophy
are projected and activated? Whichever the case be, it is clear that
violence and Auschwitz have compelled us to write and speak in
different ways. One of these is the rite that James Bernauer rescued
from oblivion: the auricular confession that Höss and Lohn articulated days before executing the former's death sentence.

Lohn's Salutation

Höss received the sacrament of penance from the Jesuit Lohn on
April 10, 1947. Bernauer introduces us to this moment by imag-
ining the Jesuit's salute. It is a brief and seemingly mere formal
moment. However, Lohn's salute is a historically forged ritual
salutation—it assumes the priest's presence at the auricular confession, mandatory since the Fourth Lateran Council (1215),[5] and
it conveys the benevolent attention of the priest requested since

---

[3]   Eric Weil, *Logique de la Philosophie* [1950] (Paris: Librairie Philoso-
phique J. Vrin, 1996).

[4]   We owe this reflection to the Chilean poet, Raúl Zurita. See Homer,
Iliad, I.1–6.

[5]   See Henry Denzinger, *The Sources of Catholic Dogma* (Fitzwilliam,
NH: Loreto Publications, 1955), no. 437.

the Council of Trent (1551).[6] More importantly, this ritual salutation is a speech act that invests Lohn as a confessor and Höss as a
penitent. As part of the penitential rite that has begun, it demands
words by Höss to confess all the acts by which he created and
managed the infernal place of Auschwitz. Thus, Lohn ends his
salute by subtly reactivating the priestly right to interrogate the
penitent by saying, "May the Lord be in your heart and on your
lips, so that you may rightly confess all your sins."

Auricular Confession

The auricular confession performed by Höss and Lohn follows
a procedure forged over centuries, emerging from a reflection
on penitential metanoia.[7] The Fourth Lateran Council and the
Council of Trent established the central elements of the penitential
mechanism carried out by the former commander and the Jesuit,
namely, the realization of a private and secret confession of the
penitent,[8] organized around three acts—contrition, confession,
and satisfaction[9]—where the priest must listen, interrogate, and
eventually absolve the penitent as a judge[10] and physician.[11] The
manufacture of this penitential mechanism should not be confused
with the effects it promises and the truth that justifies it. Auricular
confession promises to produce a peculiar alethurgy, that is, the

---

[6]   Ibid., nos. 893–906. On the priest's rights, see Michel Foucault,
Abnormal (New York: Verso, 2003), 177–80.
[7]   On this history, it is instructive to see Henry Charles Lea, *A History
of Auricular Confession and Indulgences in the Latin Church*, vol. 1 (Philadelphia: Lea Brothers, 1896) and the response by P. H. Casey, *Notes on a History of
Auricular Confession* (Philadelphia: John Jos. McVey, 1899).
[8]   Denzinger, *The Sources of Catholic Dogma*, nos. 901 and 916–18.
[9]   Ibid., no. 896.
[10]   Ibid., no. 902.
[11]   Ibid., nos. 437 and 905.

manifestation of God's and the believer's truth.[12] Such a manifestation involves the realization of a particularly complex metanoia that brings together an individual dimension, which requires instituting priests as physicians for the recovery of spiritual health, and a societal dimension, which requires priests to be judges who impose satisfaction to restore justice. Yet, the complexity of this metanoia is that it adds another dimension to the two preceding ones. We call it cosmological. In effect, through auricular confession, the believer who has broken his friendship with the divinity, and therefore with other creatures, reactivates the metanoia operated in the life of Christ. That is, he reactivates the cosmological condition for access to salvation.[13]

The Impotence of Auricular Confession

Is auricular confession, which operates through a private and fiduciary encounter of only two actors, an adequate mechanism to enable the complex Catholic penitential metanoia concerning someone confessing those events that created Auschwitz? Our question is not theological but examines the historical constitution of the auricular mechanism and its alethurgical capacity. Does it seem sufficient today (to you and me) for a penitential mechanism to be articulated through a private and secret communication before a priest, which does not consider a ritual moment to hear the cry (Ps 22; Job 3) of those exterminated or who experienced the inverted metanoia of this infernal place? Is it sufficient today (for any religious community) for a penitential rite to be capable of absolving a penitent but unable to hear or reckon with believers of

---

[12]   On alethurgy, see Michel Foucault, *On the Government of the Living* (New York: Palgrave Macmillan, 2014), 7–11, 52, 80–82.

[13]   See Council of Trent, in Denzinger, *The Sources of Catholic Dogma*, nos. 894–95; John Paul II, *Reconciliatio et Paenitentiae*, III; *Ordo Paenitentiae*, 6c; and *Notitiae* 2015/2.

another faith who inherit the extermination or survive the inverted metanoia of any infernal place? The auricular mechanism used by Höss and Lohn (not the effects it promises or the truth that justifies it) seems to us incapable of processing the societal dimension of the penitential metanoia it fosters. It is thus impotent to be a visible and effective sign (*Catechism of the Catholic Church*, no. 1127) of God's justice and grace, that is, to manifest the truth that grounds penitential metanoia.

Demands to Problematize

The impotence of the auricular confession on the infernal place of Auschwitz demands to problematize anew the mechanism of our penitential metanoia. To this end, the relationship between violence and discourse must be reconsidered philosophically. For so doing, the historical–philosophical work by Eric Weil is a particularly fruitful beginning. According to Weil, violence occupies a dual place concerning discourse.[14] On the one hand, violence precedes any discourse. On the other hand, violence activates, gives life to, and compels discourse. So insofar as all discourse on violence is historical, a new type of violence announces the expiration of those discourses incapable of containing it. The work of thought, when confronted with a new figure of violence, consists in elaborating a new discourse (category) that allows us to account for this new violence in order to strive to contain it.

---

[14]   Eric Weil, *Logique de la Philosophie*, 73–86. It is worth noting that the reflections on violence by Eric Weil, a Franco-German philosopher of Jewish descent, are deeply connected with Nazism and Auschwitz. On the one hand, his mother and sister were deported to Theresienstadt and later to Auschwitz, where they were murdered. On the other hand, Weil was a member of the French army under a fictitious name. When he was arrested, he was sent as a French soldier to a concentration camp where he developed the ideas on the connection between philosophy and violence that he would expound in his French doctoral thesis, *Logique de la Philosophie*.

At the risk of simplifying our theme, but without betraying it, this logic could allow us to analyze the historical variations of sacramental theology and its ritual demands. It also enables us to rethink auricular confession so that the violence of infernal places (such as that created in Auschwitz) can somehow be discursively articulated in a penitential rite. Accepting this latter task does not entail dreaming of a penitential discourse liberated from history but accepting the challenge that the present imposes on penance: to manifest the promised penitential metanoia through the penitential mechanism when it is more needed, namely, when a Catholic creates and manages an infernal place such as Auschwitz.

Conclusion

We have raised a question about the potentiality or impotence of the auricular confession vis-à-vis the creator and manager of Auschwitz. To answer this question, we qualified Auschwitz as an infernal place and described the Höss–Lohn auricular confession as a ritual to contain the violence deployed there. After briefly outlining the historical constitution of the auricular of confession employed by the former Commandant and the Jesuit, we then differentiated the auricular mechanism from the effects it promised and the alethurgy it aimed to manifest. Our provisional conclusion was that the present auricular mechanism was incapable of ushering in the complex penitential metanoia promised and, therefore, that this mechanism found a limit in the infernal place of Auschwitz. This recognition should initiate a critique of the penitential rite and its alethurgical capacity.

At this historical juncture, such a beginning should reflect on the relationship between sacramental discourse and its frailty in the face of the violence within the infernal places that we have created during the last century.

6

Political Reconciliation, Relationality, and Absolution

SERENA PAREKH

Since the Second World War and the trials that followed, apology, forgiveness, and their roles in political reconciliation have been important topics for political philosophers. The question I want to ask about an Auschwitz absolution has to do with the political implications of the confession and subsequent forgiveness. What does it mean for the world—the common world all of us must share—that Höss was absolved for his role in Auschwitz? What does it mean to live in a world where Höss can supervise the unimaginable suffering and death of hundreds of thousands of people, and then receives "the reward of everlasting life" and the "supreme gift of God's mercy" without even really acknowledging the true horror of what he has done? Following Hannah Arendt, I see these as political questions because they have to do with the common world and how we share it with others.

In contrast to Höss's story, consider another example of reconciliation. In 1993, Amy Biehl, a twenty-six-year-old woman from Newport Beach, California, was stabbed to death in a township in

South Africa. She had come to South Africa as a Fulbright scholar to support the anti-Apartheid movement. One day she found herself in the middle of a mob chanting anti-White slogans and was killed in the fray. Four men were convicted of her murder but released from prison after only five years as part of South Africa's Truth and Reconciliation Commission. Amy's parents, Linda and Peter Biehl, despite being devastated by their daughter's death, agreed to meet her killers after their release from prison. As Amy's mother Linda wrote, "It wasn't about pity or blame, but about understanding. We wanted to know what it would take to make things better."[1] Her parents developed a relationship with the men and ultimately forgave them. They went on to create the Amy Biehl Foundation Trust to discourage future violence in South African townships.

This example of forgiveness stands in sharp contrast to what unfolded between Fr. Lohn and Rudolf Höss. The four men who killed Amy Biehl reached out to her family in order to apologize and ask for forgiveness, an act that showed their genuine sense of repentance. What is so striking about Höss's confession is his lack of genuine repentance. What he thinks of having done wrong was being too "hard and too strict" and saying "many a bad word in anger," faults that many of us are guilty of. He was unable to articulate how his actions contributed to the hell on earth he helped to create at Auschwitz and as such didn't repent for it. While he acknowledges that the extermination of the Jews was wrong, he seems to have no real understanding of *why*. "It was exactly because of this mass extermination that Germany earned itself the hatred of the entire world. The cause of anti-Semitism was not served by this act at all, in fact, just the opposite. The Jews have come much closer to their final goal." Auschwitz, for Höss, was wrong because it didn't help the cause of anti-Semitism and harmed Germany's

---

[1] Linda Biehl, TheForgivenessProject.com, https://theforgivenessproject.com/stories-library/linda-biehl-easy-nofemela/.

reputation. It is hardly an expression of genuine sorrow for the suffering and destruction of life that he caused.

There is another way in which Höss's confession and subsequent forgiveness is troubling and different from the case of Amy Biehl's killers. This has to do with its political dimension and lack of attention to its impact on the common world. The fundamental difference between the reconciliations of Höss and Amy Biehl's killers has to do with what feminist philosophers refer to as the relationality of forgiveness—that forgiveness involves victims, the community, as well as the perpetrator and priest. For Kathryn Norlock, forgiveness is relational in the sense that it involves recommitting to a relationship, seeing someone in a new light and taking seriously the way that power operates in this. Because of its relational nature, it's important to be attentive to the outcomes of forgiveness that include improved relationships.[2] On the political level, a relational view of forgiveness means that we must pay attention to the ways that forgiveness shapes societies and relations between citizens, including between those who were harmed and those who did the harm. This relational understanding of forgiveness does not seem to be present in Höss's confession and absolution. In Höss's case, the reconciliation served only him and there was little sense of how it might impact his community or Germany at large. For the Biehls, forgiveness served not only the perpetrators of the crime, but the Biehl family as well as the community their daughter worked and was murdered in. They were able to transform their grief into a legacy of forgiveness and support for the communities in which the violence arose.

But it had a further consequence as well. It provided a model for an entire nation that was eager to learn how to live together— victim and perpetrator—after the horrors of apartheid. In other

---

[2]   Kathryn Norlock, *Forgiveness from a Feminist Perspective* (New York: Lexington Books, 2018).

words, it had a relational aspect that restored bonds and repaired the common world. This relationality is deeply political because it provided a way to live together after something horrific had taken place.

Given this, it's hard not to view Höss's reconciliation in a negative light. Not only did the person who created hell on earth for thousands of people himself escape hell, but those who suffered at Höss's hands and their descendants who suffered indirectly, were done a disservice. They were not offered the opportunity to reconcile and forgive. Of course, given Höss's lack of sincere repentance, it's hard to know what they would have forgiven him for, had they even been open to it. The problem with his confession and reconciliation is not that the grace was cheap, as Bonhoffer said. It's that the power of forgiveness was not used to restore the world that he destroyed. It remained purely private and purely for Höss's own sake. This is a loss for his victims and for the common world he did so much to destroy. The relationality of forgiveness was totally ignored. This is intensified by the fact that he was sorry for some parts of his actions but continued to hold the kind of world-destroying views of Jews that were the foundation of the Holocaust. If he were able to do it again, but this time successfully and while spending more time with his family (one of his big regrets), one can imagine him eagerly doing it again.

It's important to recognize forgiveness not merely as a private act between an individual and her or his confessor, but as a practice that is relational and that can have deeply political implications. As the feminist philosopher Claudia Card wrote, "evils change moral relationships among those who become perpetrators, bystanders, beneficiaries, or victims."[3] Forgiveness has the power to reshape

---

[3]   Claudia Card, *The Atrocity Paradigm: A Theory of Evil* (New York: Oxford University Press, 2002), 167.

these relationships and repair the world that was destroyed by the evil. Höss's confession and reconciliation did none of this.

Bernauer asks whether the absolution of Höss reflects a spirituality of no consequences for sinful conduct and whether it camouflages, rather than negates, sin and evil. I appreciate the acknowledgment that forgiveness has the power to do both. The desire to be forgiven for one's sins, crimes, and transgressions remains powerful. Could the church have been more aware of the impact of Höss's absolution on the common world? Could the granting of forgiveness have been done in a way that was attentive to the relationality of forgiveness and its world-repairing power? Perhaps. But perhaps that was too much to ask given how recent the war was and how little time there was before his execution. Nonetheless, attending to the way that forgiveness connects people, restores communities, and rebuilds relationships—or not—is fundamental, I believe, to political power and potential of forgiveness.

7

The Freedom of a Catholic Man?

ROBERT P. BURNS

A troubling thing about Fr. Lohn's encounter with Rudolph Höss is not that Lohn visited this condemned man and listened to his story, his confession, but that Lohn, a priest but a human being, purported to *absolve* him of his sins. The Roman Catholic practices surrounding reconciliation have changed radically over the centuries. Other Christian communities and many Christian authors, including some of the greatest of Church Fathers, have argued that the forgiveness of sins is the prerogative of God alone. Trent approved the current language of absolution, spoken by the priest in the first person singular (*"Ego te absolvo ..."*), which seems to have come into use only in the second millennium. It is hard to derive the precise contours of Catholic discipline here solely from any New Testament language without a very demanding deference to Catholic tradition, especially that part of the tradition that was shaped in opposition to modernity. The particulars of Lohn's absolution cannot be derived solely from the centrality of forgiveness in Jesus's teaching.

I am a lawyer. I suspect that Catholic canon lawyers might have plausible arguments as to whether canon law resolved the questions that faced Fr. Lohn.[1] I suspect that canon law may provide that the

---

[1]   Fr. Bernauer's engaging reconstruction of Lohn's diary seems to suggest

resolution of these issues falls within the informed moral discretion of each individual priest. If one accepts a strong version of the authoritativeness of the magisterium expressed through canon law, it would be the end of the matter. From this internal Catholic point of view, could Lohn have simply said to Höss after his confession, either "This sacrament does not contemplate atrocities such as those you presided over. I can hear your confession, perhaps I can pray that God forgive you, but I cannot absolve you in this case"; or "Given the length and depth of your adherence to National Socialism, I cannot trust my judgment about the depth of your repentance." I assume a Catholic canon lawyer might be able to answer these questions.

Catholic sensibility in the modern age has embraced a countercultural view that Catholic teaching, and the philosophical principles underlying it, is superior to even the best expressions of modernity. In a much less virulent context, consider the view, largely dominant in Catholic intellectual circles fifty years ago, that the *philosophia perrennis,* a medieval gloss on Aristotelianism, was superior to even the best modern thinking had to offer.[2] Popular versions of Catholic moral teaching, and the place of confession within it, envision a church monopoly of an almost hydraulic system of sanctifying grace. This monopolistic and hydraulic concept of the church's role has had some dark consequences. So, protecting the laity from truths about the clergy that may "scandalize" and lead them away from the sacraments becomes a transcendent imperative. This can lead to other "disastrous error[s], incompatible with the teachings of Christ."[3]

---

that canon law provides that an ordinary priest may (must?) offer absolution for any sin if a penitent is facing death.

[2] See, e.g., John Courtney Murray, *We Hold These Truths: Catholic Reflections on the American Proposition* (New York: Sheed & Ward, 1960).

[3] Michael Dyler, "A Disastrous Error, Incompatible with the Teachings of Christ," *LaCroix International,* August 9, 2022.

There are troubling things about this particular absolution. The sin from which Höss was absolved was not a single moral failure for which a person may form a "firm purpose of amendment." That kind of failure seems to be where the sacrament, understood at least in popular Catholicism, seems to find its natural home. The absolution in Höss's case seems to have extended to his actions over decades, closely intertwined with his identity as a National Socialist, and supportive of mass murder, genocide, unimaginable individual suffering, and the establishment of a total terror state. In any criminal context, Höss would have been guilty of much of the evil that the Third Reich perpetrated: millions of capital crimes. So, there is the simple enormity of the crimes. That alone might have counseled leaving forgiveness to God, even before reaching the doubts about the reliance on a particular priest's judgment of the penitent's sincerity, a kind of judgment only an omniscient God could reliably make.

Regarding that judgment of sincerity, there is the depth and length of his identification with National Socialism, an ideology that is wholly incompatible with his late profession that "the extermination of the Jews was wrong, absolutely wrong." "Wrong" is simply not an operative category: Hitler's vulgar motto was "Right is what is good for the German people."[4] Even after his late reconversion to Catholicism, Höss claims, "I am now as I was then, as far as my philosophy of life is concerned. I am still a National Socialist. A person who has believed an ideology, a philosophy for almost twenty years and who was bound up body and soul cannot simply throw it away just because the embodiment of that idea, the National Socialist state and its leaders acted wrongly." To the

---

[4]   Hannah Arendt, *The Origins of Totalitarianism* (New York: Harcourt Brace Jovanovich, 1973), 299. For the operationalizing of this notion in the Reich's courts, see Ingo Muller, *Hitler's Justice: The Courts of the Third Reich*, trans. Deborah Lucas Schneider (Cambridge, MA: Harvard University Press, 1991), 76.

last, Höss seemed to regret the final solution as "wrong, absolutely wrong" not in any moral sense (Nazism could not contemplate that sense), but because it earned Germany "the hatred of the entire world," frustrating the "cause of anti-Semitism," and bringing "[t]he Jews much closer to their final goal." That judgment seems wholly compatible with a purely National Socialist view that the final solution was wrong only because it turned out not to be "good for the German people."

From a Catholic point of view, Höss's sin in his long embrace of National Socialism seems more to involve an apostasy that always implicitly contemplated authorizing and abetting mass murder, an apostasy that he adhered to until the end. Did Lohn properly discern Höss's sincerity in both his rejection of his apostasy and remorse for the murder committed under his authority? Did the four hours they spent together allow him to make that judgment? Literature contains portraits of confessors of exquisite sensibilities that can discern the present spiritual condition of a person. Think of Fr. Zossima's discernment of the dark state of the older Karamazov's soul. There were levels of adherence to Nazi ideology, and there are levels to that ideology. Not every committed Nazi thought about all the aspects of the ideology as it was stated by its more systematic expositors. A complete version seems to have included (probably logically incompatible) naturalism or vitalism, racism, amoralism, atheism, and operationalism (the Führer's orders as ultimate). Höss embraced National Socialism for over twenty years and proclaimed himself *still* a National Socialist *after* he converted back to Catholicism. And National Socialist ideology was not simply discontinuous with a Christian worldview, as were Roman religions, but self-consciously created in opposition to that worldview.

Late in the Reich, it seems that Höss recognized two moments of possible decision[5] that might have limited the depth of evil to

---

[5]   In contrast to Höss's lack of "courage" in these instances, see the

which his long adherence to National Socialism had led him. It was not until 1941 that Höss received the order (from Himmler personally) to turn Auschwitz from a concentration camp into an extermination center, with all the additional misery and despair that brought even to the (still) living. The extent to which his apostasy had become "corruption," a "crime against the Holy Spirit," seems apparent in his response: "[T]he reasoning behind the order of this mass annihilation seemed correct to me. At the time I wasted no thoughts about it. I had received an order; I had to carry it out." Questioning the Führer "was beyond my frame of mind ... there was no second guessing for an old National Socialist, much less an SS officer." And two years later, after he was promoted to a position in Berlin, he chose to return to Auschwitz "to preside over the murder of almost one half million Jews."

The Gospel tells us that God is forgiving, even when the motivation for repentance, as in the Prodigal Son parable, is less than pure ("Even paid workers in my father's house have more than I do."). And yet there are other difficult passages in which it is suggested that even God can or will not forgive certain sins ("sins against the Holy Spirit")—suggesting that these sins involve a *continuing, indeed a permanent,* change in attitude toward God, not simply an individual failure. Did a twenty-year embrace of National Socialism and an ambiguous rejection of the final solution suggest just that?

---

account of the conscientious refusal of Franz Jägerstätter to be inducted into the German army in an unjust war, a decision that cost him his life. Alan Donagan, *The Theory of Morality* (Chicago: University of Chicago Press, 1977), 15–17. Donagan believes this example shows the validity of distinctively moral judgment, in opposition to what he takes to be Hegel's view, even against the current "ethical" consensus. Donagan notes ruefully that the Catholic bishop who tried to dissuade Jäggerstätter said after the war that Jäggerstätter was a hero to conscience, "but to an inculpably erroneous conscience" and that it was the "heroes" of the *Wehrmacht* who "conducted themselves ... in the light of a clear and correct conscience" (ibid., 16).

In a conversation some years ago with accomplished lawyers who were also Christian believers, we discussed the question, "Does God care about the facts?" Some maintained that God cares only about the quality of the believer's *current* disposition that the freedom of the sons of God before God allows for freedom from whatever the facts about past behavior might be. Before God, we are never reducible to our past acts.

That's not the way we usually make moral and legal judgments. I am acquainted with a form of moral and legal evaluation that is close to common sense, the common law trial. We believe that an excruciatingly detailed—and adversarial—analysis of the facts of a case is the best way to determine a defendant's state of mind at the time of an alleged crime, and resolve the inevitably forward-looking judgment about the appropriate judgment to be made now. Here, the judgment about a defendant's present deserts is very closely intertwined with, perhaps almost identified with, precisely what he has done. Now this device allows, when it works, for a very refined, legal judgment, necessary for maintaining a legal and moral order, but perhaps not a more ultimate judgment by a forgiving God. The New Testament suggests that God is ultimately forgiving of a soul that may abjure all of the deeds that our common-sense institutions say define a person's character. Höss's case, it seems to me, places that possibility in realms of mystery[6] beyond what any human institution, even church institutions, can embody. Perhaps the best that can be said of Lohn's absolution is that it was only the promise of the possibility of forgiveness for a soul that only God could ultimately judge.[7]

---

[6] For an account of Kierkegaard's understanding of individual salvation by faith wherein "[s]alvific possibility is neither immanent in the self's actuality nor a continuous projection of the self's past," see Mark C. Taylor, *Journeys to Selfhood: Hegel & Kierkegaard* (New York: Fordham University Press, 2000), 252–61.

[7] Of course, traditional Catholic doctrine provides that absolution brings only forgiveness, not impunity, as Dante's *Purgatorio* illustrates.

8

Auschwitz Absolution

A Confessor Reflects in Fear and Trembling

David Neuhaus, SJ

Prior to ordination, my imaginings about my priestly role focused on celebrating the Eucharist, preaching on the Word of God, and working with the marginalized. It was only in the last year of my studies that hearing confessions began to occupy my thoughts, when like all prospective priests I was required to take a course focused on this subject known as *ad Audiendas*. Canon 970 of the Roman Catholic Code of Canon Law (CCL) states, "The faculty to hear confession is not to be given except to priests whose suitability has been established, either by examination or by some other means."

After ordination, I enthusiastically embraced this part of my ministry, confident that Christ, working through the priest, turns sin into an occasion for renewed communion with God through the church. Keenly aware of how unworthy I am to serve as mediator of God's absolution, I rely on knowing the condition of the validity of the sacraments is not my worthiness but God's mercy, preeminently manifested in Christ's death for us sinners on the cross. Since that time, I have heard not only the confessions of sweet old ladies or confused adolescents. I also served as a prison chaplain in a high security prison where I encountered people who had murdered, a few in cold blood. It was a formative experience to witness contrition, listen to confessions, and grant absolution. I understood, as I insisted that penitents should, too, that absolution does not turn the clock back. It cannot restore what has been destroyed: even the most contrite penitents remain legally responsible for the harm they had done.

I have never been in a situation where a mass murderer asked me to hear his confession. I believe that instinctually I would turn away, forced to admit to myself—and perhaps even confess this as a sin—that I am unwilling to be a channel of God's mercy in the face of crimes so heinous that absolution not only seems unthinkable but obscene. That instinct protests vociferously: how can such a man receive absolution? Surely justice demands that so monstrous a man be abandoned beyond the reach of God's mercy! Yet perhaps this is precisely the issue at stake. Is Höss beyond the reach of God's mercy?

Jesus does declare that one sin cannot be forgiven: the enigmatic sin against the Holy Spirit: "whoever blasphemes against the Holy Spirit can never have forgiveness, but is guilty of an eternal sin" (Mk 3:29). This sin refers I think to turning one's back on the Holy Spirit, the very source of forgiveness. By blaspheming the Spirit, the sinner blocks the possibility of forgiveness. In his brazen request to have his confession heard, Höss did not blaspheme the Spirit. Having actively participated in the murder of millions, he was then turning to God. Three moments are essential in this process: Höss's determination to go to confession, Lohn's readiness to hear the confession, and the pronouncement of absolution.

Canon 987 of the CCL states, "To receive the salvific remedy of the sacrament of penance, a member of the Christian faithful must be disposed in such a way that, rejecting sins committed and having a purpose of amendment, the person is turned back to God." It is the penitent's contrition that brings him or her to the confessional. In the memoirs he was encouraged to write while in prison, Höss described with cold precision the orders he had received to plan and execute the Final Solution. In his detailed retelling of life in the death camp, there is no small degree of self-justification and little palpable contrition. But in his last letters to his wife and children, written mere days before his execution, Höss expressed more remorse and recognized that he had been the cog in the wheel of enormous evil. Contrition, however heartfelt, does not set the past right, but it can reorient the future.

In Höss's case, the known future was the gallows to which he was led two days after his confession. There he died without protest, accepting that he was a war criminal, without shirking his responsibility. What did his confession change? By putting words to his crimes, he provided the most chilling description we have of the evil humanity is capable of. Perhaps, he also prepared himself to meet his Maker. In his final statement sent to the Polish state prosecutor on April 11, 1947, six days before his execution, Höss said, "May the facts which are now coming out about the horrible crimes against humanity make the repetition of such cruel acts impossible for all time."[1]

Lohn was available to hear Höss's confession; I cannot imagine that I would have been. Is it permissible for a priest to turn away a penitent who seeks to enter the confessional? The CCL states, "All to whom the care of souls has been entrusted in virtue of some function are obliged to make provision so that the confessions of the

---

[1]   Höss's statement quoted by John Jay Hughes, "A Mass Murderer Repents: The Case of Rudolf Höss, Commandant of Auschwitz." The Archbishop Gerety Lecture at Seton Hall University, March 25, 1998, https://www.shu.edu/theology/upload/mass-murderer-repents.pdf.

faithful entrusted to them are heard when they reasonably seek to be heard and that they have the opportunity to approach individual confession on days and at times established for their convenience.... In urgent necessity, any confessor is obliged to hear the confessions of the Christian faithful, and in danger of death, any priest is so obliged" (Canon 986). As a Pole, a Catholic, a Jesuit priest, Lohn would have always been aware of the tens of thousands of Polish Catholics, laypeople, religious, and priests executed at Auschwitz. By the time of the confession, he would have also known that millions of others had perished under the supervision of Höss.

Lohn had the quasi-impossible task of judging whether Höss was indeed sufficiently contrite. How much contrition is enough? Canon 978 states, "In hearing confessions, the priest is to remember that he is equally a judge and a physician and has been established by God as a minister of divine justice and mercy, so that he has regard for the divine honor and the salvation of souls." What serves the divine honor and the salvation of souls in such a case? Canon 980 makes clear that "if the confessor has no doubt about the disposition of the penitent, and the penitent seeks absolution, absolution is to be neither refused nor deferred." It seems unthinkable that absolution could be granted in this case! Yet is this not at the heart of the scandal of the Crucified One: God's mercy does not balk even in the face of the most atrocious human evil. God does not allow evil to have the last word.

Central to the rite of confession is the penance defined by the confessor for the penitent. The Roman Catholic Rite of Penance explains penance: it "may suitably take the form of prayer, self-denial and, especially, service to neighbor and works of mercy. These will underline the fact that sin and its forgiveness have a social aspect" (*Ordo Paenitentiae* 18). The CCL states, "The confessor is to impose salutary and suitable penances in accord with the quality and number of sins, taking into account the condition of the penitent. The penitent is obliged to fulfill these personally" (Canon 981). The carrying out of the penance is a condition for effective absolution. "True conversion is completed by expiation for the sins committed, by amendment of life and also by rectifying injuries done" (*Ordo Paenitentiae* 8c). The expression "rectifying injuries done" is scandalously inadequate in the face of the enormity of Höss's crimes. What penitence might Lohn impose on Höss two days before his execution? Would that Höss be obliged to gaze unswervingly until the end of time, into the faces of the men, women, and children, Jews, gypsies, Jehovah witnesses and homosexuals, Poles, and others he had murdered.

What happens in the confessional is between the penitent and God, even if mediated by the confessor. The penitent can only come to confession fully conscious of the loss of God's favor due to sins committed, sins that when remembered provoke the sinner to seek the restoration of that grace of God and reintegration into the church. The consequence of a true confession is the outpouring of mercy from God and reconciliation with the church. This religious act, however, does not constitute a juridical act. The responsibility of the penitent for his or her acts remains in force. Indeed, confessing to God as a penitent involves taking responsibility for the consequences of sin. God does not forgive in place of the victims.

It is humanly nauseating to think that Höss might have died at peace with God and church, but it is unbearable to believe that as Höss turned to God, what he had done might escape God's inexhaustible mercy.

9

The "Absolution" of Höss

A Contemporary Catholic View

WALTER F. MODRYS, SJ

In October 1960, John F. Kennedy stood before a bank of Baptist ministers to defend his candidacy as a Catholic running for president of the United States. The charge against him was that a Catholic president could not exercise the constitutionally required freedom from Vatican control of American policy. The Baptists, schooled in the Catholic teaching of the day, outmatched Kennedy on the point. Formal Catholic teaching at the time, though largely disregarded in practice, still reflected the outdated political thinking of the nineteenth-century social order in Europe. Accordingly, the church traditionally claimed a privileged position in the political life of the nation. Only later, at the Second Vatican Council in the mid-1960s, would the church revise its teaching on freedom of conscience and the legitimate independence of the secular order, demonstrating once again that the teaching of the Catholic Church can change, adjusting to new circumstances and understandings.

I was reminded of this precedent and the inadequacy of church teaching at a particular moment when I read the dramatic story of Fr. Władysław Lohn's soul-searching postwar encounter with Rudolf Höss, the former Commandant of Auschwitz. No seminary course or theological treatise of the time could have prepared Fr. Lohn for the moral and spiritual quandary he faced when meeting a penitent complicit in the murder of millions of innocent victims. The common practice and teaching on "confession" never anticipated such a sin being brought forward in the confessional. Fr. Lohn, somewhat like Kennedy thirteen years later, was largely on his own to find the right way to proceed in the tumultuous conflict with Communist regimes and the conflicting moral exigencies and the spiritual crisis he faced in the attempted annihilation of the Jewish people.

This is not the place to expound in detail on the revisions of "confession" in Catholic theology since the time of Fr. Lohn. And it may be the case that these theological advances have still not permeated today's Catholic attitudes and practices as much as they should. Yet, for present purposes, it is hoped that the discussion below of Catholic progress in theology and practice may prove fruitful as a guide to further reflection. First, much of the church's changed understanding is suggested by the change in nomenclature from "confession" to the "sacrament of reconciliation." In the celebration of this sacrament, the act of confessing one's sins to a priest has come to be understood as only one of the elements of the sacramental ritual, and one can argue, it is not the primary element. By instituting this change in the late 1960s, the church was implementing the teaching of the Vatican Council by no longer explicating the action of the sacrament in largely legalistic terms. The previous pre–Vatican II approach has now been recognized as inadequate and potentially misleading.

Yet we can imagine that the confession of Höss is what engaged the full attention of Lohn at the time and indeed so tweaks our natural curiosity today. But this interchange between priest and penitent is something we will never discover because of Lohn's strict adherence to the privacy seal of confession. Nevertheless, from today's Catholic perspective, the religious focus should not be on what Höss said in confession (what possibly could he have said?), but on the action of divine grace and the openness to that grace by the penitent, however he or she expresses it. Bonhoeffer's critique of "cheap grace" was on target against the abuses that the previous legalistic understanding of the sacrament was prone to succumb to.

Catholics sometimes thought that simply saying your sins to the priest could make them disappear, almost magically. Of course, this was never the church's true intention nor an accurate description of its formally approved theology. But the post–Vatican II directives served as a much-needed corrective to the popular devotions and practices. The grace of the sacrament is acknowledged as a gratuitous gift of God. It is not merited through the penitent's stance before the priest functioning as his judge. Neither the penitent's action nor the priest's response is the source of divine grace. This is an important change in understanding not just because it relegates the legal aspects of the granting of absolution to a more constricted context of protecting against abuses, but even more because it injects a faith-filled spiritual core—the redemptive action of Christ—into the sacramental celebration.

In such a theological understanding, the notion that Fr. Lohn's granting of absolution is the church's judgment on the significance of his crimes or the expiation of his guilt must yield to a more theologically accurate assessment. Absolution is the formal declaration of the church to stand with a fellow sinner, enclosing him or her within the community of the church whose mission is to serve as an instrument of divine reconciliation in the world. It is not an endorsement of the sinner's reformed character or his rehabilitation or the recompense he has paid for his sins. In short, it is not some kind of stamped card issued by a juridical official that one can present to the divine judge, constraining God's freedom to act in line with his supernatural justice and mercy.

The cited declarations that "Rudolf Höss is now in heaven" because he was absolved of his sins are therefore rash and unfounded. None of us dies with that kind of presumptive assurance. Better to leave aside those kinds of pronouncements and far better to rely on God's mercy and the efficacious power of divine grace routed in Christ's redemptive action on our behalf, the best and surest hope we can have. There are sins, genocide certainly being one of them, that seem to surpass the human capacity to forgive. We sometimes glibly project onto God the same incapacity, based on our own notions of justice and accountability. Some sins, we insist, cry out to God, sins even God cannot forgive without compromising his self-proclaimed righteousness. Such impassioned protests need to be balanced against the complex portrait that the scriptures present of divine dispositions toward the unfaithfulness of ancient Israel and sinfulness of human kind.

Yet it is not just in religion where we confront this unavoidable complexity. For we are plagued, even in our politics and systems of criminal justice, with the dilemma when forgiveness or pardon or amnesty seem the only ways to avert continuing bloodshed and evil, while extending forgiveness and pardon may expose us to the risk of failing to convict the evil doer and impose on him or her the penalty that justice calls for. One thinks, for example, of the reconciliation process led by Nelson Mandela after the fall of Apartheid in South Africa. Did the Truth and Reconciliation Commission that he created, despite efforts to respect the accountability to which the guilty must be called, nevertheless result in many guilty perpetrators escaping the just penalty they deserved in justice? We presume so, because no human effort is infallible and the commission was surely an imperfect remedy. Yet we all admit that at times, only forgiveness, as imperfect as its granting may be within ordinary human affairs, is a moral imperative.

Höss was not forgiven for his crimes against humanity, nor did he deserve to be, even if we were to gloss over the obviously imperfect nature of his contrition. The church judges that it can legitimately take his sins to the judgment seat of God and pray that the redemptive death of Christ will be extended even to the point of somehow embracing the horror of his actions. In doing so, the church does not discount the accountability divine justice requires for his sins. The final judgment—how all this fits together—is not subject to our decree, either as a faith community or a civilly commissioned authority.

These are some of the questions the church of today must grapple with, as must we all, regardless of our religious faith or affiliations. For in these matters, we confront ultimately the mystery of good and evil, of justice and mercy, the perfect resolution of which must always allude us. There is some evidence that Fr. Lohn spent the rest of his life wrestling with the decision he made. Certainly, few of us, or perhaps none of us, will ever face the moral and spiritual dilemma that confronted him. And yet, despite the tragically catastrophic features that confronted the priest, when we are fully alert to the deepest significance of human affairs, all of us must feel a kinship with this deeply conflicted Jesuit.

10

The Karmic Debts of Rudolf Höss, Mass Murderer

FRANCIS X. CLOONEY, SJ

A Murderer's Enlightenment—
And Lingering Bad Karma

The *Middle Length Sayings* (*Majjima Nikāya*) is a Buddhist sacred text, a collection of ancient stories about and teachings of the Buddha. In it there is a chapter called the *Aṅgulimāla Sutta*—the story of Aṅgulimāla. Aṅgulimāla was a frightening bandit and murderer. Very violent, he was a gruesome collector of fingers, making a garland by taking one finger from each of those he murdered and stringing them all around his neck: thus, his name, which means "Garland of Fingers." The Sutta tells us that he had fashioned a grisly garland of 999 fingers and, when he saw Gautama, the Buddha, he saw him merely as a potential one-thousandth victim, whose finger would complete his murderous garland. The decisive scene is this:

> Then Aṅgulimāla saw the Blessed One coming from afar and on seeing him, this thought occurred to him: "Isn't

it amazing! Isn't it astounding! Groups of ten, twenty, thirty, and forty men have gone along this road, and even they have fallen into my hands, and yet now this contemplative comes attacking, as it were, alone and without a companion. Why don't I kill him?" So Aṅgulimāla, taking up his sword & shield, buckling on his bow and quiver, followed right behind the Blessed One. Then the Blessed One willed a feat of psychic power such that Aṅgulimāla, though running with all his might, could not catch up with the Blessed One walking at normal pace. Then the thought occurred to Aṅgulimāla: "Isn't it amazing! Isn't it astounding! In the past I've chased and seized even a swift-running elephant, a swift-running horse, a swift-running chariot, a swift-running deer. But now, even though I'm running with all my might, I can't catch up with this contemplative walking at normal pace." So he stopped and called out to the Blessed One, "Stop, contemplative! Stop!" "I have stopped, Aṅgulimāla. *You stop.*"[1]

And so Aṅgulimāla suddenly stops, no longer travels his murderous path. The Buddha was not afraid of him, and by refusing fear and refusing to fight or flee, he broke the cycle of violence. He converted the bandit who became his disciple and was received into the monastic life.

The Buddha sent him forth as a monk, telling him to present himself as sinless and blameless—not despite his past life, but because, from the moment of his conversion he became a disciple

---

[1] *Aṅgulimālā Sutta*, translated from the Pali by Thanissaro Bhikkhu, http://buddhasutra.com/files/Buddhist_Sutra_A2.pdf. See also the use of the story of Aṅgulimāla by Michael Barnes, SJ, in "Living Interreligiously: On the 'Pastoral Style' of Comparative Theology," in Francis X. Clooney and Klaus von Stosch, *How to Do Comparative Theology* (New York: Fordham University Press, 2018), 301–23.

and a new person, his evil deeds left behind as the residue of a person who no longer existed. The 999 murders no longer need burden him.

But seeing Aṅgulimāla as it were only from the outside, other people recognize him merely as the same feared and hated bandit:

> Then Ven. Aṅgulimāla, early in the morning, having put on his robes and carrying his outer robe & bowl, went into Savatthi for alms. Now at that time a clod thrown by one person hit Ven. Aṅgulimāla on the body, a stone thrown by another person hit him on the body, and a potsherd thrown by still another person hit him on the body. So Ven. Aṅgulimāla—his head broken open and dripping with blood, his bowl broken, and his outer robe ripped to shreds—went to the Blessed One. The Blessed One saw him coming from afar and on seeing him said to him: "Bear with it, brahman! Bear with it! The fruit of the kamma that would have burned you in hell for many years, many hundreds of years, many thousands of years, you are now experiencing in the here-&-now!" Then Ven. Aṅgulimāla, having gone alone into seclusion, experienced the bliss of release.[2]

In principle the Buddha does not approve of such revilement—since the Aṅgulimāla who had committed all the wicked deeds is no more—yet he does observe that by suffering now, Aṅgulimāla saves himself from suffering in various hells after death, before rebirth in this world.

There are numerous texts in Hindu and Buddhist traditions that recount how the deeds of any given birth are rewarded or punished in temporary hells and heavens after death, and then in new births—better or worse than the previous birth, depending on

---

[2]   *Aṅgulimālā Sutta*, translated from the Pali by Thanissaro Bhikkhu.

how much evil had been done previously. For example, the code known as *The Laws of Manu* (*Mānava Dharma Śāstra*) lists hells fitting to various crimes. But worse still are the new bodies into which one is born, as one deserves. Some of these are catalogued in *Manu* XII:

> Those who commit grievous sins causing loss of caste first go to dreadful hells during large spans of years; upon the expiration of those, they reach the following transmigratory states: A murderer of a Brahmin enters into the wombs of a dog, a pig, a donkey, a camel, a cow, a goat, a sheep, a deer, a bird, an [untouchable] Cāṇḍāla, and a Pulkasa. A Brahmin who drinks liquor enters the wombs of worms, insects, moths, birds that feed on excrement, and vicious animals.... By stealing grain, one becomes a rat; by stealing bronze, a ruddy goose; by stealing water, a Plava coot; by stealing honey, a gnat; by stealing milk, a crow; by stealing sweets, a dog; by stealing ghee, a mongoose. (XII. 54–56, 62)[3]

Evil action can be ended and karmic effects not yet activated can be stifled, but karmic effects already under way must be lived out and exhausted over time, in this world or by postmortem punishments and long cycles of rebirth through many lesser bodies before another human birth.

Those who slaughter the innocent will in turn be slaughtered, due to their own crimes, sooner or later, as punishment and on the path of purification. The idea of punishments in an intervening hell or in a vile new body commensurate with the crimes committed balances perceptions of imbalance in this life, and may well appeal to the sense of justice and fairness of onlookers. Grace, insofar as

---

[3]   *Manu's Code of Law*, trans. Patrick Olievelle (New York: Oxford University Press 2005), 233.

such is involved, means that deeds will not entirely annihilate evildoers, but rather set them on a course in which they pay their debts and make amends in their own suffering now, in afterlives, and in further lives on earth.

Rudolf Höss' Absolution— And Karmic Residues

These examples come to mind as I think about the case of Rudolf Höss. What are we to make of the fact that Fr. Władysław Lohn, SJ, heard Höss's confession just days before Höss was executed, perhaps letting a scoundrel gain forgiveness—from God if not from humans—and escape retribution by easy words of repentance just before death?

Höss's horrific crimes make us balk at the idea that he might go to confession and be absolved, forgiven, and restored to grace. Even if we believe in the efficacy of sacramental confession, it seems too easy, and wrong, considering the genocide he facilitated, so carefully, knowingly, coldly, for so very long. We cannot even be sure whether he was sorry—or for what. Even when he admits that massacring the Jews was wrong, the error lay in the fact that the atrocity was a strategic error, provoking hatred for us, gaining sympathy for them, advancing their aims:

> Today I realize that the extermination of the Jews was wrong, absolutely wrong. It was exactly because of this mass extermination that Germany earned itself the hatred of the entire world. The cause of anti-Semitism was not served by this act at all, in fact, just the opposite. The Jews have come much closer to their final goal.[4]

---

[4]   Rudolf Höss, *Death Dealer: The Memoirs of the SS Kommandant at Auschwitz* (New York: Da Capo Press, 1996), 183.

This shows no human regret for the murders or Christian repentance for the hatred. Could we have blamed Fr. Lohn had he
refused to come to the prison to hear the confession of the doomed
murderer or having come, refused absolution to Höss, if it were
clear that he was not truly repentant of his sins?

But just as Aṅgulimāla's murders, suffering, and liberation
must be considered in the context of Buddhist thinking on karma,
we need to consider the Catholic context in which the confession
took place. We must step back and consider how Höss's last-minute
confession would be interpreted in light of how pre–Vatican
II Catholics thought about sin, punishment, and redemption.
Presumably, Höss himself, though a fallen Catholic, thought in
those traditional terms, even after Nazism became his "religion."
Presumably Lohn, too, thought in terms of the Catholic calculation of sin, forgiveness, and satisfaction operative in that era. What
then might we learn from sources as authoritative as the Council of
Trent or the Catechism of Peter Canisius?

In Book I of its explication of the Apostles Creed, the *Catechism of the Council of Trent* (the *Roman Catechism*, 1566), when
treating of Article V, "He descended into hell, the third day he rose
again from the dead," lists three destinies after death: a permanent
hell, a permanent heaven, and a temporary purgatory:

> These abodes are not all of the same nature, for among
> them is that most loathsome and dark prison in which
> the souls of the damned are tormented with the unclean
> spirits in eternal and inextinguishable fire. This place is
> called gehenna, the bottomless pit, and is hell strictly
> so-called.
>
> Among them is also the fire of purgatory, in which
> the souls of just men are cleansed by a temporary punish-
> ment, in order to be admitted into their eternal country,
> into which nothing defiled entereth. The truth of this

doctrine, founded, as holy Councils declare, on Scripture, and confirmed by Apostolic tradition, demands exposition from the pastor, all the more diligent and frequent, because we live in times when men endure not sound doctrine.

Lastly, the third kind of abode is that into which the souls of the just before the coming of Christ the Lord, were received, and where, without experiencing any sort of pain, but supported by the blessed hope of redemption, they enjoyed peaceful repose. To liberate these holy souls, who, in the bosom of Abraham were expecting the Savior, Christ the Lord descended into hell... The souls of the just, on their departure from this life, were either borne to the bosom of Abraham; or, as is still the case with those who have something to be washed away or satisfied for, were purified in the fire of purgatory.[5]

The post-mortem fate of an absolved Höss would fall into the second of these categories, escape from damnation, but a consignment to the fires until cleansed.

In his *Summa Doctrinae Christianae*—surely known, at least in German translation, to every German Catholic of Höss's generation—St. Peter Canisius devotes several paragraphs of his treatment on the Sacrament of Penance to the satisfaction due for sins already forgiven.[6] Paragraph IV.8 defends the idea of satisfac-

---

[5] As found online, page 58 in the online version of the Catechism, at https://saintsbooks.net/books/The Roman Catechism.pdf. Or, for a slightly different translation, *Catechism of the Council of Trent*, trans. J. Donovan (Dublin: James Duffy, 1914), 55–56.

[6] See Peter Canisius, *Catechismi Latini et Germanici. Catechismus Maior, Prima Pars: Catechismi Latini*, ed. Frederick Streicher, SJ (Rome: Pontifical Gregorian University, 1933), 137. See also my treatment of the *Catechism* in Chapter 3 of Francis X. Clooney, *Reading the Hindu and Christian Classics: Why and How Deep Learning Still Matters* (Charlottesville: University of Virginia Press, 2019).

tion after death; IV.9 identifies purgatory as a place where such satisfaction is achieved through suffering there. Some biblical figures, such as Abraham, Isaac, and Jacob, seem never to have sinned. Some, such as David, Ezekiel, Peter, Magdalene, sinned, but they did sufficient penance in this life. But most people, even those who will reach heaven, die with satisfaction still due, and must pass through purgatory, suffering until they are ready for heaven. It is in the third group that Höss would be placed.

The fact that Lohn heard Höss's confession meant only that he was forgiven, so as to be saved from damnation. Satisfaction for his sins, severe punishment—in this life by execution, and in purgatory after death—would still be required. There is nothing to suggest that Höss did not have to pay for his sins; he was almost certainly—as far as we can tell from afar—not ready for heaven at the moment of his execution. Although he suffered after capture, as did Aṅgulimāla, it seems obvious that by the logic of pre–Vatican II understandings of sin and expiation, he had much more to expiate after death. Höss's sacramental confession, understood in accord with the norms of the pre–Vatican II church, cannot be taken to indicate that once absolved, Höss would go immediately to heaven. He surely would have known this, if any shred of the Catholic faith remained in his mind.

One other factor is the obligation probably felt by Fr. Lohn, who could not simply pick and choose whose confessions to hear, whose to reject. He was perhaps like Fr. Sebastian Rodrigues in Martin Scorsese's *Silence* (itself based on Shūsako Endō's novel of that name). He, too, may have felt duty-bound to administer the sacrament, not out of a personal inclination to be kind and to forgive, but rather because (as even today) a priest does not get to choose when to invite the sinner into God's mercy. But it is just as certain that he would not have imagined that he was sending Höss straight to heaven. He was not opening the gates of heaven to Höss but only closing the doors on hell. Satisfaction, punishment in this life and after death, retained their place.

What of Höss himself? Even if he knew the teaching of Trent and of Canisius in some popular form, what fragments of Catholic imagination did he retain? In his memoir, written in the days before his death, Höss does not come across as vividly Catholic. He almost never introduces stories or images from Catholic piety. Jesus is never mentioned, and thus, too, neither his crucifixion nor our redemption by his death. Mary is not named nor any of the saints. His few references to "God" make one wonder how far he had drifted from any manner of Catholic piety, even from youth on. Perhaps confessing his sins was a mere formality? We cannot tell. Perhaps he thought he would confess and get right into heaven? We cannot tell. But we can be sure that the church of the 1940s would likely have dismissed out of hand the notion that an absolved Höss would enter heaven immediately.

Can We Reassess the Confession— In Our Imaginative Space?

I began this reflection by pointing to the Buddhist story of Aṅgulimāla, his wickedness, conversion, suffering, and enlightenment. I used that story to give us a space in which to think of the ending of sin and the conversion of the wicked but also the ensuing penalties that had still to be suffered even by a truly repentant person.

Can we imagine taking seriously, as a 1940s Catholic would have seen things, the existence of purgatory—place, state, period of time—and the fairness of a dying person falling into purgatory even after confession and absolution? Can we ask how long the Commandant of Auschwitz should remain in purgatory to atone for his leading role in the death of well over a million and the suffering of so many more? It we could imagine all this, it would be helpful. Although we cannot really ask how long Höss stayed in purgatory—a "place" outside of space, a time beyond time—the idea that Höss, though not damned, suffered after death could attenuate our indignation that he might seem to have gotten away with millions of murders.

But, if truth be told, most of us do not inhabit and perhaps cannot even visit or revisit that old Catholic cosmology. Most of us do not think in accord with the categories of heaven, purgatory, and hell, just as most of us do not live in a world where the consequences of deeds are tabulated in terms of karmic residues. We cannot easily factor in the idea of purgation after death, and expect judgment in the here and now of this life. To say that Höss's confession saved him from hell but not from "a very long time in purgatory" might well have been convincing after the war, when Höss confessed to Lohn. But if we are thinking about how to treat abhorrent murderers in this life alone, the idea of postmortem satisfaction probably will not satisfy us and not help us to forgive the sinner. This means that we may also not be able to understand Höss's confession or how Höss and Lohn thought about the confession.

Yet revivals of old ideas and images are possible. Pope Benedict XVI sought to reinterpret the image of purgatory and satisfaction after death in several paragraphs of his 2007 Encyclical *Spe Salvi* (*In Hope We Are Saved*). Consider this effort to reimagine purgation after death as an encounter with Christ:

> Some recent theologians are of the opinion that the fire which both burns and saves is Christ himself, the Judge and Savior. The encounter with him is the decisive act of judgement. Before his gaze all falsehood melts away. This encounter with him, as it burns us, transforms and frees us, allowing us to become truly ourselves. All that we build during our lives can prove to be mere straw, pure bluster,

and it collapses. Yet in the pain of this encounter, when the impurity and sickness of our lives become evident to us, there lies salvation. (no. 47)

All Fr. Lohn could do was to clear the way, such that Höss would finally meet Christ, beyond the gallows:

> At the moment of judgement we experience and we absorb the overwhelming power of his love over all the evil in the world and in ourselves. The pain of love becomes our salvation and our joy. It is clear that we cannot calculate the "duration" of this transforming burning in terms of the chronological measurements of this world. The transforming "moment" of this encounter eludes earthly time-reckoning—it is the heart's time, it is the time of "passage" to communion with God in the Body of Christ. (no. 47)

In the end, there is a wonderful balance, justice and grace together:

> The judgement of God is hope, both because it is justice and because it is grace. If it were merely grace, making all earthly things cease to matter, God would still owe us an answer to the question about justice—the crucial question that we ask of history and of God. If it were merely justice, in the end it could bring only fear to us all. The incarnation of God in Christ has so closely linked the two together— judgement and grace—that justice is firmly established: we all work out our salvation "with fear and trembling" (Phil. 2:12). Nevertheless grace allows us all to hope, and to go trustfully to meet the Judge whom we know as our "advocate," or *paracletes* (cf. 1 Jn. 2:1). (no. 47)[7]

---

[7] https://www.vatican.va/content/benedict-xvi/en/encyclicals/documents/hf_ben-xvi_enc_20071130_spe-salvi.html.

Encounter with Christ, full and complete after death, would then be *the* efficacious event of purification, and confession merely a route out of this world, which would enable Höss finally to stand unprotected and vulnerable for Christ. If so, we may end up thinking once more of Aṅgulimāla who was saved from his accumulated evil not by the Buddha's word but by encountering the Buddha. It was that encounter, not a theory of karma or freedom from karmic residues, that made him suddenly leave his evil ways and become a disciple of the Buddha. It seems that no such encounter with Christ brought Höss to a halt during the years of his Nazi leadership or even in the period just before his execution. Perhaps, facilitated in this life by Fr. Lohn's hearing his confession, that encounter would come after Höss's execution: "the decisive act of judgement," that encounter with Christ that burned, transformed, and freed Höss, allowing him to become truly himself.

11

The Priority of Interhuman
Confession and Reconciliation

Ruth Langer

Many years ago, in a day-long retreat introducing Christian-Jewish relations and dialogue, I presented an overview of the multifaceted negative teachings, often leading to violence, that shaped the history of our communities, culminating in the Shoah. Afterward, many of the Christians approached me, tearfully pleading for forgiveness. My response? No. And why not? Because as someone not personally harmed by these atrocities, I was not in a position to forgive. Even more so, were I a victim of the atrocities, I could be asked to forgive the perpetrators, but those Christians who approached me were personally innocent. In Jewish tradition, formal forgiving is not the appropriate mode for reconciliation between those removed from the events. Our repaired relationship will find expression instead in our building together a world that learns from its past errors and sins and seeks, through education and action, to prevent their recurrence. This would be a genuine substantive act of communal penitence.

Indeed, as has been well explored, especially in Simon Wiesenthal's *The Sunflower* and elsewhere, while forgiveness does play a role in Jewish practice, it is something that is operative between penitent sinners and their victims, and only once achieved there, between the sinner and God. God does forgive all or almost all sins provided that the sinner is truly penitent, demonstrating this first by verbal confession both to the human victims and to God, and then by genuine attempts to make amends for the sin. For more heinous crimes, the rabbis teach, divine forgiveness does not necessarily come immediately or without first undergoing suffering. In extreme cases, complete atonement occurs only with the sinner's death, provided the sinner was truly penitent.[1]

How might this apply to the case of Rudolf Höss? In Jewish understanding, God's forgiveness is readily available for sinners who are truly penitent. Such people have confronted the depths of their sinfulness and determined that when faced again with the same situation, they would not repeat this sinful behavior. The Hebrew word *teshuvah*, from the root "to turn," involves a complete turning away from the sin committed and toward a life according to God's will. This process, performed as completely as humanly possible, is a nonnegotiable prerequisite to asking for and receiving God's promised forgiveness.

Did Höss really repent? Bernauer, speaking through Lohn, wonders precisely about the quality of Höss's penitence. As he notes, there are huge gaps in his confession. He seems to have no remorse for eliminating Jews. He finds excuses for his behavior, explanations that attempt to avoid responsibility for his own actions, shifting blame to those above him and those below him,

---

[1]   A classic summary of this is Maimonides, *Mishneh Torah*, Laws of Repentance, especially chap. 1 and 2:9–10. https://sefaria.org/Mishneh_ Torah,_Repentance.1.1?lang=bi&with=Translations&lang2=en. Heinous crimes explicitly include desecration of God's name, and, implicitly, any category of crime traditionally punishable by death, whether imposed by human courts or directly from God. There is substantial debate in the literature he summarizes about what sort of sin fits into what category.

but never accepting that he himself had agency. Rather than an actor who chose to participate in this evil drama and even shaped his own role within it, Höss presents himself as simply an obedient cog in the Nazi machinery.[2] He dehumanizes himself, even as he dehumanized his victims. As a machine, without choices, he suggests, sin is not even a valid category.

Perhaps, as Lohn seems to have concluded, the quality of a confession is not entirely for us humans to judge. Yet, the Catholic practice of confession to and absolution via a priest places a burden on the priest, a third party to the sin, to make precisely this discernment. Granted, the ideal priestly role embeds significant elements of spiritual direction, of helping the sinner toward a more complete penitence. However, on a deathbed, on the eve of an execution, this process is necessarily cut short, and the pressure to offer absolution following a confession must be intense. One can only wonder what the process might have looked like had this interaction taken place without the threat of the gallows, had Lohn (or perhaps a psychologist) met with Höss regularly over years, helping him toward a moral adulthood, to a person God would forgive, not out of mercy, but because he had so thoroughly reformed himself.

But Höss's confession took place in prison on the eve of his execution in private communication with Lohn. There was no opportunity for extraliturgical acts of penance following his absolution. In Jewish understanding, though, demonstration of penitence must precede receiving divine forgiveness. Such penitence cannot avoid direct interface and repairing relationships with the people harmed. Höss's surviving victims would have been the ones who could best grant him the human forgiveness necessary to this process. As Maimonides writes (2:9), sinners have an absolute obligation, before turning to God, to make amends to and beg the forgiveness of the person(s) harmed, seeking to demonstrate

---

[2]   See Lohn's diary in Part One of this volume.

the authenticity of their remorse. If they fail to appease their victims, the sinners need to try again, up to three times, bringing along three others, presumably to testify to the authenticity of the sinner's remorse in a quasi-judicial setting (three adults form a rabbinic court). Only after this, too, has failed may the sinner turn directly to God without completing this human-level repair. The sin then becomes that of those failing to be appeased and forgive, says Maimonides.

Höss did not address his victims directly, the situation in which in Jewish understanding such a confession must take place to underline its sincerity and allow repair of relationships. The privacy of the confessional, a privacy crucial to his understanding of the validity of the process,[3] separates contrition and penance in a way foreign to the Jewish system. For a public meeting of this sort to happen, though, in 1947, was virtually unthinkable. The agitating of unhealed wounds, the trauma involved in such a confrontation, is grotesque to contemplate. That some Jewish survivors might have been willing to testify at a trial is plausible but that would not have been a setting for reconciliation. It is highly unlikely that survivors of Auschwitz would have been ready to accept the authenticity of the penitence of the person in charge of their suffering. Given the extreme nature of the sin involved, given Höss's lack of insight into his own guilt, I cannot criticize them or consider this a theoretical sin on their part.

There are additional relevant considerations: if the victims are no longer alive, as was the case for millions here, the sinner must go to their graves, confess, and verbalize his penitence there. In this case, it was utterly fitting that Höss's execution took place at Auschwitz. But was his confession, his expression of penitence, voiced to the camp's victims? His final declaration of guilt speaks

---

3   See Höss's discussion in Part One of his childhood experience of violation of the privacy of the confessional.

specifically only of his Polish victims, perhaps because he was tried by Poland. His confession itself is laced with anti-Semitism, with the sense that somehow destruction of the Jews was justified. When he admits that the destruction of the Jews was "wrong, absolutely wrong," he explains that this is because the method did not prevent the Jews from achieving their final goal—unspecified here but presumably something like the world domination of the anti-Semitic canard.

Höss's confession was neither voiced at his victim's graves nor was it spoken to the souls of his victims. For those familiar only with biblical Judaism, this last may sound like a strange statement, but by the rabbinic period, Judaism had come to an understanding that humans do have eternal souls, souls that separate from the body after death and go, perhaps after some months of purgation in Gehenna, to God. But these souls maintain a relationship to their bodies, too, and in traditional Jewish belief, the two will be reunited and return to resurrected life on earth in the messianic resumption of Jewish national life. Therefore, intact burial of the body was also important—and therefore, the Nazi cremation of bodies and denial of this burial was an added desecration. It is only in contemporary times, among Jews with discomfort with the supernatural elements of this belief, that other funerary practices have been deemed acceptable—sometimes explicitly in solidarity with Hitler's victims.[4] For many though, Auschwitz-Birkenau is one enormous cemetery, specifically connected to the souls of its victims. A confession there would have been spoken to his victims.

However, this all presumes that the sinner has genuinely and completely repented. In Höss's case, it is very clear, especially in his continued slighting of his Jewish victims and in his shifting of the blame, that the survivors and the surviving Jewish community

---

[4]   For a short summary, see "Jewish Views on Cremation," https://www.myjewishlearning.com/article/judaism-on-cremation/.

would be entirely justified in doubting his remorse and his reform. In that case, especially given the enormity of his crimes, it is legitimately beyond the human capacity to forgive. Does God forgive? The Talmud (b. RH 16b–17a) teaches that wholly wicked people, Jews and gentiles, who die unrepentant suffer in Gehenna for a year and then cease to exist. However, the most wicked remain suffering in Gehenna for eternity, and "even were Gehenna to cease to exist, they would not." Who invokes upon themselves such a curse? This includes, most notably, communal leaders who lead others astray.

12

Unforgivable Sins

KENNETH SEESKIN

Since confession is the issue under discussion, I can think of no better way to open this essay than with a confession of my own. I read Professor Bernauer's imagined diary of Father Lohn with interest, and though I disagree with the decision to grant Höss absolution, the diary raises the right questions and offers evidence of a tortured soul.

But I read the Höss confession with utter revulsion. It opens by suggesting that he was the victim (my comrades and subordinates disappointed and deceived me) rather than the millions of people who were tortured, degraded, and murdered at the camp he ran. What was he thinking when millions of men, women, and children were stripped naked and herded into gas chambers? At no point does he seem to understand the full nature of the horror he perpetrated. Though he offers an apology to Poles, his contempt for Jews is undiminished. In fact, his final admission is that the killing of Jews was wrong because it made Germany look bad and therefore "The Jews have come much closer to their final goal." I saw no mention of the Roma, the handicapped, homosexuals, or other groups who perished there.

Rather than give Höss more attention than he deserves, I would like to take up the issues raised in Fr. Lohn's diary.

Unforgivable Sins

Both the Hebrew Bible and the Gospels recognize the category of an unforgivable sin. According to Deuteronomy 29:17–19, if a person, clan, or tribe turns away from God to worship the gods of other nations thinking they will be safe and avoid punishment, God will never forgive them and will blot out their names from under heaven. In the same way, Matthew 12:31–32 (cf. Lk 12:10, Mk 3:28–30) says that while blasphemy against the Son of Man will be forgiven, blasphemy against the Holy Spirit will not be forgiven either in this age or the age to come.

Blasphemy is a hard thing to define. Does the systematic degradation of creatures made in the image of God constitute blasphemy against God? Ditto for idolatry. I suggest that rather than stick with these categories, we substitute the category of radical or irredeemable evil. On this issue, the Christian theologian John Hick has written:

> These events [Auschwitz and Belsen] were utterly evil, wicked, devilish and, so far as the human mind can reach, unforgivable; they are wrongs that can never be righted, horrors which will disfigure the universe to the end of time, and in relation to which no condemnation can be strong enough, no revulsion adequate.[1]

I would add to this that no extenuating circumstance or attempt at restitution is anywhere near adequate. The fact is that when we are dealing with this kind of evil, the categories we use to describe

---

[1]   John Hick, *Evil and the God of Love* (New York: Palgrave Macmillan, 2007), 397.

normal transgressions, for example, lying, stealing, promise breaking, even some cases of murder, no longer apply. What would it mean to compensate a victim of Nazi cruelty—even if such "compensation" extended to a heavenly abode?

I have argued that attempts to rank or compare instances of irredeemable evil are misguided.[2] Cold-blooded murder is a worse crime than manslaughter; but when we get to the death camps, or the Gulag, or the killing fields of Pol Pot, comparisons serve no purpose. In short, we reach a point where our moral categories break down. Even the most graphic descriptions fall short of the true nature of the horror we are contemplating. So, while it may be the case that God's infinite mercy can accommodate the perpetrators of such events, I agree with Hick that as far as the human mind is concerned, these sins are unforgivable. I am not saying that there is a hard and fast distinction between forgivable and unforgivable sins, only that the latter is a legitimate category.

Following Orders

A standard reply of those accused of committing moral atrocities is that they were just following the orders of their superiors. It is no secret that military, religious, and political authorities often demand unquestioning obedience and that those under them regard it as a virtue to meet their demand. It is worth noting, however, that God, the ultimate authority, never asks for this. No protest can be heard when Abraham (Gn 18:23) and then Moses (Ex 32:11–13, Nm 14:13–17) hold God to account. Rather than a set of marching orders, the laws given at Sinai are presented as a pact (*brit*), entered into by God and Israel. The people are given

---

[2]   Kenneth Seeskin, "What Philosophy Can and Cannot Say about Evil," in *A Holocaust Reader: Responses to Nazi Extermination*, ed. Michael L. Morgan (New York: Oxford University Press, 2001), 321–32.

ample opportunity to think it over and decide if they really want to stay committed. The prophets compare it to a marriage vow. Since it is up to humans to determine how to interpret and apply the terms of the pact, it would be best to say that as depicted in the Hebrew Bible, revelation is a participatory process.[3]

To carry this idea a step further, the Hebrew Bible leaves no doubt that military, religious, and political leaders can be and often are corrupt. Pharaoh is portrayed as the ultimate villain. Ahab, Manasseh, and Jehoiakim were scarcely better. God tells Jeremiah to go to war with priests, prophets, and kings alike. From a biblical perspective, then, the "just following orders" defense is hollow. Whose orders are you following? What do these orders ask you to do? No doubt refusing to follow orders can result in punishment, humiliation, or death. But all are preferable to obedience to an evil regime. Even if one is serving a legitimate regime, any attempt to stop thinking and act in a completely subservient way amounts to a denial of one's status as a moral agent and is never justifiable.

Repentance

Whatever their differences, Judaism and Christianity agree on the importance of repentance. Not only is repentance encouraged, both traditions assign it transcendental importance. The Talmud (*Berakhot* 34b) teaches that where the penitents stand, not even the righteous can stand. Jesus expresses the same sentiment at Luke 15:7. The question is, how do we know when repentance is genuine?

First there must be a full confession. In Judaism, a private confession may be enough for sins committed against God, but it is

---

[3]   For further explanation of the participatory nature of revelation, see Benjamin D. Sommer, *Revelation and Authority: Sinai in Jewish Scripture and Tradition* (New Haven, CT: Yale University Press, 2015), 1–3, 31, 42–44, 52, 241, 248–50.

not sufficient for sins committed against other people. For the latter category, one must feel remorse, go to the person who has been wronged, confess the wrong, and suffer whatever embarrassment or loss of esteem may follow. I realize that not every religion follows this practice. But given the public nature of the crimes committed at Auschwitz, surely some sort of public apology was needed.

According to Moses Maimonides, even a public apology is not enough. If a man has had improper relations with a woman, he must be alone with her, be able to repeat the act, and refuse not out of fear or weakness but because he has had a change of heart.[4] Granted that Maimonides is talking about a paradigm case of repentance that may be difficult for most people to emulate. Still, he has made a valid point. Performing the rituals governing repentance is not enough unless one has undergone a fundamental change. The problem now becomes, how do we know when such a change has occurred? How do we know that the motivation behind an act of repentance is genuine and not that the person wants to escape punishment or maintain a sense of self-esteem?

While Maimonides's test would provide strong external evidence for such a change, even that may not be sufficient. An unrepentant sinner can keep up appearances without feeling a tinge of remorse. The answer to the question of how we know that the motivation behind an act of repentance is genuine is that, strictly speaking, we cannot. As the Bible tells us (1 Sm 16:7), only God looks into the heart. I take this to mean that while we must do our best to assess the sincerity of the penitent—perhaps according the penitent the benefit of the doubt—we can never be certain how the penitent will appear in the eyes of God.

To return to the specifics at hand, one can question how successful "Denazification" was in Germany and how many SS officers "repented" to save their own skins. To apply Maimonides's

---

[4]   Maimonides, *Mishneh Torah* 1, Laws of Repentance, 2.1.

principle, if they were given the chance to serve again in circumstances similar to the ones that obtained when Hitler came to power, would they refuse and be willing to suffer the consequences? Although we will never know for sure, there is ample room for doubt.

Conclusion

It should be clear by now that I do not support Fr. Lohn's decision to grant absolution. I have nothing to go on except general principles and indirect evidence. I do not doubt that God's mercy is infinite and may exceed the limits of human understanding. My objection to the granting of absolution would not be as firm if all Lohn had done is called upon God's mercy and left the matter in God's hands. While some may view this as a shirking of his priestly authority, I do not. Faced with evil that defies human comprehension and a woefully inadequate expression of remorse, he could have asked for mercy but refused absolution. One could object to even this much.

The fact is, however, that he went further: "I absolve thee from thy sins in the name of the Father and of the Son and of the Holy Ghost." If this means that God is required to absolve the sinner as well, I would ask how anything we do on earth can possibly bind God. To repeat, only God looks into the heart. If, on the other hand, it means only that Lohn performed his duties as a priest but that the final decision still rests with God, I think he erred by giving the penitent the benefit of the doubt in a case where the grounds for doubt were considerable.

13

Is Absolution Possible
for Genocide?

DAVID BIALE

We might safely dispose of Höss's confession as laughable, if the stakes were not so high. He whines about his subordinates keeping him in the dark about what, we may assume, were evil actions attributed to him. He laments how his single-minded focus on his job froze his emotional availability to his family, all the while neglecting to mention that his job was dedicated to murdering other people's families. And, while he allows that perhaps genocide was the wrong tactic to use on the Jews, he doesn't waver for a moment from adherence to an anti-Semitic ideology that sees all Jews—no matter how young or old—as the enemies of Germany.

No, if we were looking for a good case study of how confession to genocide might lead to absolution, Höss's would scarcely qualify. But the question remains, what, if anything, might absolve a genocidal criminal of his crime? In these brief remarks, I will not consider the Catholic context of Höss's confession, but rather examine how the Jewish tradition might approach the question.

It must be noted at the outset that Judaism has no sacrament of absolution for those who confess their sins, but confession is nevertheless widely endorsed in Jewish texts. The Shulchan Arukh, the law code from the sixteenth century that remains the operative basis of *halakhah* (rabbinic law) promises entry to the "world to come" to those who recite a deathbed confession (*vidu'i*), a ritual already established by tractate Semachot of the Talmud. Confession had a recognized place in Jewish liturgy, quite apart from deathbed confessions, and the great legal scholar Moses Maimonides drew the distinction between sins between a person and God, which must be confessed privately, and sins regarding another person, which may be confessed publicly.

Confession is but one part of the larger practice of repentance (*teshuvah*), which has a very high status in Jewish culture. The penitent is seen as greater than a righteous person and Jewish legend (*midrash*) holds that God created repentance before he created the world. Rabbi Eliezer taught that one should repent one day before one dies, thus linking such repentance implicitly with a deathbed confession. When his disciples pointed out that one cannot know the day of his or her death, Eliezer replied, "All the more reason to repent today, lest one should die tomorrow."

How one should repent and to whom are subjects that the Jewish sources treat extensively. Following the destruction of the Temple, sacrifices no longer provided the vehicles for atonement, but the rabbis substituted good works, such as charity, for animal sacrifice. And, if someone sinned against his or her fellow humans, then asking forgiveness or making recompense became essential parts of the process of *teshuvah*.

There is no evidence in Höss's confession that he even remotely understood what might constitute *teshuvah* in the Jewish sense. One might have expected him to make a direct appeal to the surviving family members of his victims to forgive him or at least to acknowledge to them his consciousness of the evil that he committed. But we search in vain for any such self-awareness.

Repentance in the Jewish tradition is linked to God's attribute of mercy. But mercy is always balanced by the attribute of justice. Thus, while God might forgive a sin against him, justice demanded punishment for those who committed sins against their fellow humans. Moreover, there are circumstances in which repentance is deemed impossible: "Anyone who makes the many sin is not given opportunity to repent" (*Mishna Avot,* v, 18), something of which Höss, as Commandant of Auschwitz, was surely guilty.

In tractate Sanhedrin 7a of the Babylonian Talmud, we read that the killing of a priest or prophet in the Temple is "a crime that has no repair (*tikkun*)." The rabbis clearly regarded such a murder as being in a different category than other homicides. We might ask ourselves whether the crime of genocide is similarly "a crime that has no repair." When Adolf Eichmann was sentence to die for his central role as Jewish "specialist" in the Holocaust, there were those who called for him to be put to hard labor instead and contribute to the building of the Jewish state. Surely, such a punishment would have constituted a kind of *teshuvah*, making recompense to those whose families he conspired to murder. But if genocide is a "crime that has no repair," then perhaps the death sentence was the only appropriate punishment, even for those otherwise in principle opposed to capital punishment.

Here, I would turn from the ancient rabbis to the philosopher Hannah Arendt, who argued in her *Eichmann in Jerusalem* that the crime of genocide is qualitatively different from murder multiplied by millions of times. Genocide not only deprives its victims of their lives, but it is also crucially "an attack on human diversity as such, that is, upon a characteristic of the 'human status' without which the very words 'mankind' or 'humanity' would be devoid of meaning."[1] Since, for Arendt, nations as cultural communities that

---

[1]   Hannah Arendt, *Eichmann in Jerusalem: A Report on the Banality of Evil* (New York: Penguin Books, 2006), 268–69.

differ from each other are essential aspects of nature, genocide is therefore a crime against the order of nature, namely, the naturally diverse condition of the human race.

It is genocide defined in this way that justifies the death penalty for *génocidaires*. Arendt ends the epilogue of her book with an imagined speech by the judges to Eichmann upon his sentence, a speech that we might equally imagine relevant to Rudolf Höss:

> And just as you supported and carried out a policy of not wanting to share the earth with the Jewish people and the people of other nations—as though you and your superiors had any right to determine who should and should not inhabit the world—we find that no one, that is, no member of the human race, can be expected to want to share the earth with you. This is the reason, and the only reason, you must hang.

14

Forgiveness and Self-Knowledge in the Imagined Case of Höss's Confession

Marina Berzins McCoy

Philosophers who have written on the topic of forgiveness have often argued about what the conditions are that warrant forgiveness. For example, Charles Griswold in *Forgiveness*[1] suggests that among these necessary conditions are an agent acknowledging responsibility, repudiating the deeds, expressing regret, demonstrating an understanding of the damage done, and offering a narrative that demonstrates a desire to change. Griswold's account makes good sense of the kinds of actions and the sorts of affective and cognitive states that we ordinarily want in situations of interpersonal forgiveness. For example, we ordinarily want not only for a person to admit that his or her action was unethical, but to experience the appropriate emotional response. For a minor instance of wrongdoing, we hope that the wrongdoer who is penitent

---

[1]   Charles L. Griswold, *Forgiveness: A Philosophical Exploration* (New York: Cambridge University Press, 2007).

will experience not only regret, but the right amount of regret. If I briefly exchange harsh words with a friend because I am tired, my regret might appropriately be relatively small, especially if the words were not especially hurtful. If I physically harm or emotionally traumatize another, my regret ought to be significantly larger. At the same time, the very admission of regret, sorrow, and a desire to change also ought to inform *how long* I ought to experience such sorrow. Most people would not want a person to feel guilty about a relatively minor outburst of irritation years later, but they might expect that even after an act of forgiveness, a degree of sorrow or regret might continue for more heinous actions.

In the Catholic tradition of confession, some elements are present while others are a radical departure from the above model. The penitent person is called to conversion as part of their reconciliation with Christ (*Catechism*, no. 1423).[2] The penitent verbally expresses sorrow, and the hope is for there to be an appropriate interior sadness, an "affliction of spirit" and "repentance of heart" (*Catechism*, no. 1431). Such conversion is interior but also exteriorized through verbal confession, acts of penance, and sacramental absolution. As Bernauer notes in his introduction, self-knowledge is an essential element of authentic repentance and conversion. A key difference in the Catholic understanding in comparison to secular accounts is that in the Catholic sacramental act, the priest is not forgiving on his own behalf, but rather is united in love to God's own forgiving action. He is "not the master of God's forgiveness but its servant" (*Catechism*, no. 1466). God's forgiveness is unconditional because its source lies not in any human ability to sympathize, but rather in God's own loving and merciful nature. Human beings can participate in that divine love but may be do so conditionally, insofar as their own love or understanding is limited.

---

[2]   References to the Catechism are to the authorized text *Catechism of the Catholic Church* (Vatican City: Libreria Editrice Vaticana, 1994).

Nonetheless, God's mercy is not thereby lessened, and the sacramental action is efficacious.

I want to look in greater detail at the question of the adequacy of self-knowledge, since Bernauer reconstructs the narrative of Rudolf Höss's own self-understanding from his memoirs. Even if we take for granted that an agent who has done wrong is genuinely sorry, there is a potential problem with self-knowledge in many cases of forgiveness. To be able to be contrite, and appropriately so in both affect and in action, requires a degree of accuracy in understanding ourselves and our own actions. But what happens if a contrite person's narrative account of his or her own actions is not adequate to the reality of the situation? For example, what if a moral actor is contrite but for the wrong reasons? Or what if he or she is sorrowful but lacks the appropriate amount of sorrow—not necessarily through its total absence but through a lack of sufficient understanding of the harm that has been enacted? Moral actors may also possess an inability to move from cognitive to affective understanding, that is, they can intellectualize or even wrongly justify themselves, even in a context where genuine sorrow is present. In other words, self-knowledge and its relation to the other interior movements that constitute forgiveness can fail in many ways.

Höss's confession, as Bernauer has reconstructed it, is rich and complex. On the one hand, the confession includes elements of genuine interior conversion. Höss admits that what he did was wrong, and he puzzles over both himself and over the actions of others who reacted differently than he had anticipated to living in the concentration camp. On the other hand, elements of his imagined confession continue to express a degree of self-centeredness and even paranoid narcissism. Bernauer suggests that a rush to forgiveness in order to put one's past behind oneself may express a "cheap grace" that stands in contrast to God's own justice.

Höss, for example, recognizes that the actions at Auschwitz were monstrous. But early on he also asserts of himself, "I was never cruel, nor did I let myself get carried away to the point of mistreating prisoners." He rues the fact that he was too "unsociable" and did not spend enough time with his family. Höss often circumvents getting to the heart of his sinfulness as an Auschwitz commander. Moreover, at the very moment that Höss states that his actions were "wrong, absolutely wrong," he also states that the goals of Nazi anti-Semitism were not well served by this approach and that the "Jews have come much closer to realizing their final goal," in effect, reasserting a hateful and paranoid anti-Semitism. Just as we as readers hope to hear the depths of human sorrow and a genuine conversion to the good, we find continued and startling distortions in Höss's thoughts and feelings. Thus, we see that self-knowledge and accurate self-narratives, while in principle desirable, may often fall far short of what we might desire of others.

We can and must wrestle with this question of self-knowledge in both its epistemic and affective dimensions. If we are the ones seeking forgiveness, we ought to be the kinds of people who are self-critical and attempt actively to question our own motives and narrative accounts of the world. However, there are at least two other epistemic elements that are not captured in a focus on the *moral actor's* self-knowledge alone. We must also consider the community that surrounds the moral actor, for example, those who survive in the years and decades after such monstrously evil actions have ended. For members of such a community are also not perfect knowers, with access to perfect justice or idealized mercy. They, like the person seeking forgiveness, also live in a state of imperfect human knowing.

We who exist as part of the larger community also lack the fullness of knowledge and self-knowledge. Our own understanding of the interior state of another person is always limited. While the narrative accounts of others, as well as nonverbal communication—such as gestures, tears, facial expressions—can partly communicate the interior state of another person, these actions always require interpretation. And our hermeneutics are always limited. To use Gadamerian language, we are always interpreting not only texts from within the horizon of our own experience but also other persons. The knowledge that we human beings bring to such interpretation is not divine, but rather always leaves us as imperfect human interpreters. To a degree, other persons and their motivations remain mysteries. We can read the words that Höss wrote in his April 12, 1947, declaration, but what we make of those words depends on us as well as on he who wrote them. As a result, any judgments that we make, whether formally or informally, must be tempered by our own self-knowledge, that is, knowing that we do not and cannot fully know the heart of another.

In fact, a good reminder of our own lack of capacity to adequately judge others lies precisely within the lived reality that we ourselves are constantly in the same situation of being judged correctly or incorrectly, adequately or inadequately, by others. Moreover, we also lack self-knowledge with respect to our own sin, contrition, and conversion. Perhaps it would be too much to say that we are all identical to a person such as Höss whose sins are manifestly evil in the extreme; to say otherwise undermines the horror of the Holocaust. Still, if we keep in mind that ordinary German citizens also often remained silent rather than protesting the Nazis, and recognize that such situations continue to happen today in a variety of political contexts, we ought not to be too sure that we are not ourselves silently complicit in real evil. Jesus advises, "Do not judge, or you will be judged. For in the same way you judge others, you will be judged, and with the measure you use, it will be measured to you" (Mt 7:1–3). This recommends to us that we remember our similarity to other sinners rather than our dissimilarity, a constant theme of Jesus's teachings. Jesus repeatedly insists that it is the contrite sinner, and not the Pharisee, to whom God draws nearest in mercy and intimacy. One reason may be that sinners who know themselves at least recognize that it is not their own good works, but rather God's own nature as love that is the source of being lovable.

From a Christian standpoint, there is also a second significant epistemic limit that we face: we cannot fully comprehend the mystery of the depth of God's mercy and forgiveness. Our lack of understanding is not merely cognitive but also emotional: not to always be able to understand God's mercy is something that we feel in our sinews and bones. Again, biblical passages are replete with cases of human indignation at God's mercy and generosity: the elder brother in the story of the prodigal son who is resentful of his younger brother's loving reception by their father (Lk 15:25–28), the real upset of Pharisees at Jesus's eating with sinners and tax collectors—who were often also part of systematic oppression (Mk 2:16), or even the anger of fellow laborers working in a vineyard who witness the field owner pay the same amount to those who show up to work at the last moment (Mt 20:1–16). God's mercy is not only tender but radical. This radical nature of God's mercy inevitably challenges us. God's mercy is not something that we always accept like a gentle restorative breeze. Rather, God's mercy can be hard to bear, at least until we allow it to carry us, rather than be guided by the limits of our own human mercy.

My own parents, grandparents, and great-grandparents were Latvian refugees who survived Stalin's terrors while some other family members died in cattle carts or in Soviet gulags. Trauma is real, and forgiveness is not an easy answer to the reality of trauma; healing requires much more. I do not know whether my grandparents or great-grandparents ever forgave the Soviets, nor would I personally burden them with this as an additional moral requirement; sometimes to be able to heal and to live is all that is possible, and we ought not burden victims with the further burden of redeeming their oppressors. God's action is to restore, heal, and to love victims and survivors. However, this is precisely why the sacramental love at work in confession and reconciliation remains essential. A priest, such as Fr. Lohn, who is acting not in his own person but as God's servant, can do what might in any given moment be impossible for a particular individual.

However, mercy itself can be nonetheless transformative. It is not the case that a moral actor's conversion, repentance, sorrow, or self-knowledge leads to God's mercy. It is really the other way around: God's love and mercy make possible all the rest. In his real-life statement, Höss wrote, "I was shown a human compassion that I never expected and which shamed me profoundly." This healthy shame, in which mercy melts away many of the obstacles to repentance, arises from encountering God's love. God's agency is the primary mover, and our own response to it secondary. For this reason, I think, more than any other, our human responsibility is always to try to accompany God in God's actions of healing and mercy, and to open new channels through which this mercy may flow.

This is not to say that human justice or judgments ought to be ignored in the acknowledgment of mystery. We can and must have institutions, such as criminal courts, that make the best decisions that they can in light of what we know or think we know. However, we might also notice that no amount of human justice heals the pain experienced in significant instances of real evil. Forgiveness may not always satisfy, but neither does Höss's execution for his crimes remove the horror of his heinous actions or the suffering of those who endured them or survived to speak of them. But this points not to a problem with justice or with forgiveness but with evil itself. As Fr. Michael Himes of Boston College once said in a campus lecture, evil is a mystery that cannot be comprehended. No justice can ever "overcome" or "blot out" the suffering and loss of millions of lives in concentration camps; if it did, it would not be true justice, for justice remembers rather than forgets. The suffering of survivors is also not always adequately healed in a lifetime, though I do believe that God can make a beginning at it.

Neither would I want to suggest that the demand for forgiveness is one that must be met in a particular way at a particular time. Forgiveness is not simply a moral demand, but rather a process that requires we recognize human limits both when forgiving and when we find ourselves unable to do so. We may find ourselves, like the elder brother in the Parable of the Prodigal Son, locked in our own human limits. Here, God is patient with us. In the parable, the father responds to his eldest son's anger by reassuring him of his love—"My son, you are here with me always; everything I have is yours" (Lk 15:31)—God assures us that when we in our own humanity cannot bring ourselves to forgive, God still loves us, too. God's nature is love and mercy. Human beings are also called, from the Christian standpoint, to also join Jesus in being agents of that mercy. What is not said enough is how radical, challenging, and hard it is to do so.

The truth is that God's mercy cannot be understood at all if it is reduced to the forgiveness of sins alone. God's mercy is a facet of God's love, a love that manifests itself through healing, creating, redeeming, and by suffering along with those who suffer, in solidarity. God suffers with us. God suffers with others whose suffering we cannot touch, heal, or relieve. Even when it seems humanly impossible, our faith is staked on the idea that God heals, loves, and continues to act to create good, and always to bring new life into the world.

Knowing that God suffers with us also can lead to a transformation of the people who allow themselves to suffer in solidarity with others. As Dorothea Sölle writes, "What matters is whether the suffering becomes our *passion*, in the deep double sense of the word."[3] Passion in this dual sense of something undergone or suffered, and in the sense of being a deep commitment, can arise from connecting deeply with God's being-with the world in its lived reality. However, we are not gods, and certainly not God. We cannot bear the burden. Whatever forgiveness looks like, it must always take account of our own humanity. Thankfully, God's love is greater than our own ability to bear or to transform evil. The question of forgiveness only becomes meaningful in the larger field of God's creative and transforming love and the mystery of that love for we who are his finite beloveds.

---

[3]   Dorothee Sölle, *Suffering* (Philadelphia: Fortress Press, 1975), 125.

15

Binding and Loosing

The Search for Penitential Practice
Adequate to Grave Scandal

BRUCE T. MORRILL, SJ

"Repent," the Gospels of Matthew and Mark recount, is the first word Jesus of Nazareth proclaims as he undertakes his prophetic mission in Galilee. This call he couples with the announcement that the kingdom of heaven, or reign of God, "has come near" (Mt 4:17, Mk 1:15). From the start, Christianity is a matter of call and response—the call coming from a God intent on finally ("The time is fulfilled," Mk 1:15) bringing the world into proper order, a project nonetheless enlisting the committed participation of people. At the outset of his Acts of the Apostles, Luke recounts how Peter's lengthy proclamation of salvation in Christ to the Jerusalem crowds on the Day of Pentecost elicited their cry, "What should we do?" Peter's answer, "Repent," to which he adds, "and be baptized every one of you in the name of Jesus Christ so that your sins may be forgiven; and you will receive the gift of the Holy Spirit" (Acts 2:38).

At the origins of Christianity, and thus the church, the gospel message is one of repentance (Greek, *metanoia*), baptism, and life guided by the grace of God (the Holy Spirit). Yet even amidst the eschatological urgency characterizing the New Testament period, the decision for repentance proved to be not a single act of repentance but a lifelong exercise in conversion from sin (*metanoia*). Baptism, it turned out, did not simply settle things, but, rather set believers on a continuous journey of converting to the gospel, as participants in a world-saving mission dependent on God and reliant on one another in community to live according to the fact of their baptism. The life of the church, in its members and as an evolving societal institution, has entailed two millennia of struggles theologically understood in terms of divine grace striving to work through human nature. Still, with the reign of God turning out to be only just arriving in a world in need of reordering, not least in and among the baptized themselves, Christian practice has entailed multiple tensions between justice and mercy, compassion and correction, capital and minor wrongdoings (in Roman Catholicism, mortal versus venial sins), the individual and the communal (in modernity, private versus public), and more. Those tensions often reach such attenuation as to constitute painful problems at given moments, some even consequential for history.

While several of those tensions pervade James Bernauer's imaginative project, his introductory chapter, to my reading, betrays his especially agonizing over the matter of justice versus mercy in the case of Fr. Lohn's pastoral ministry to Commandant Höss. Bernauer grapples with the conflicted situation through enlistment of New Testament passages conveying the boundless forgiveness Jesus instructs his disciples to practice but also the couple of verses wherein he empowers them, going forward, to bind or loose (forgive or not) the sins people have committed. Yet, the heart of the matter for Bernauer, I propose, may be further

grasped in terms of a Catholic moral-theological concept he does
not invoke, namely, scandal. Scandal, in Catholic tradition,[1] is a
matter of persons, especially those with influence in communities
or authority in social institutions, so behaving, speaking, or demonstrating an attitude as to lead others to do evil. By deed or omission
such persons (and likewise societal laws, fashions, or opinions)
tempt people's virtue and integrity and, in so doing, may cause
them to adopt similar gravely offensive thinking and behavior.
Those who use their power in a community or society in ways that
induce others to do wrong are not only guilty of scandal but also
responsible for the evil they directly or indirectly encourage.

In his Preface, Bernauer describes the Höss–Lohn affair as
an event largely unknown and never before critically examined.
In his Introduction, he reports how Lohn shared the experience
shortly after it occurred with his Jesuit community "informally and
in confidence." Following Bernauer's methodological lead, I make
this conjecture: Lohn, in addition to guarding the church's invi-
able seal of confession, may at that time have wanted to keep the
entire affair as quiet as possible so as to avoid provoking scandal,
given the postwar mixture of attitudes about the Nazis, the nature
of their crimes, the human status of Jews, and the moral obligations or culpability of the wider population. In any event, I find
Bernauer, now in the twenty-first century, pondering possible
scandalous aspects of the Archdiocese of Krakow's and Lohn's
handlings of the entire affair—accommodating Höss's request
for a priest, Lohn's absolving him of his sins, his ministering Holy
Communion to Höss and thereby readmitting him to full membership in the Catholic Church, plus some other priest reciting the

---

[1]   "Respect for the Souls of Others: Scandal," in *Catechism of the Catholic Church*, 2nd ed., nos. 2284–87 (Vatican City: Liberia Editrice Vaticana,
2019), 551. Key biblical passages, among others, enlisted in this essay include
Christ's words in Matthew 18:6 and Luke 17:1.

prayers for the dead at Höss's gallows. One senses that for Bernauer
all of this entails a grave problem of the right ordering (justice)
operative in the Roman Catholic Church on which rides its very
credibility or scandalousness, that is, its ability morally to lead and
influence, not only among its adherents but in wider society. The
problem is grave in the wake of the Nazis' systematic program for
exterminating the Jewish people and the troubled, often disastrous
history of churches, Catholic and Protestant, in relation to European Jewry and, more pointedly, the Third Reich. One can sense
also Bernauer's concern for the credibility or scandalousness of the
Society of Jesus of which he and I are members.[2]

Recounting Lohn's devotion to the Sacred Heart, a Jesuit
tradition fostering unconditional love for sinners, as well as the
Polish Shrine of Divine Mercy, Bernauer fairly acknowledges key
influences on the priest's pastoral approach to confession and
absolution. Bernauer nonetheless presses the (perhaps scandal-
countering) question of justice. Noting that the Risen Christ's
conferral of the Holy Spirit empowered his disciples not only to
forgive sins but also to "retain" them (Jn. 20:22–23), he protests:
"Whose sins should not be forgiven, should be retained? Should
the crimes of Auschwitz be retained?" The context of Bernauer's
quandary is the modern (sixteenth-century forward) Roman
Catholic sacrament of penance, wherein the climax is the priest-
confessor's passing judgment on the nature of the sin(s) confessed
and the sincerity of the penitent's contrition, including manifest
resolve, relying on God's grace, to avoid the sin(s) going forward.
The history, however, of how the early church came to interpret
the power to bind or loose a believer's sin (see Mt 16:19, 18:18)
can bring further critical light and reforming possibilities to the
problem, especially since two of the three capital sins subject to

_____

   2   See James Bernauer, SJ, *Jesuit Kaddish: Jesuits, Jews, and Holocaust
Remembrance* (South Bend, IN: University of Notre Dame Press, 2020).

binding and loosing were apostasy (publicly renouncing the faith and thus, the church) and murder.

During the first few centuries, the church fathers came to identify the power of binding not simply with the particular sin committed, but rather with the initial, public ritual (liturgical) step of a lengthy and rigorous penitential process, for which the final step was reconciliation with the church community.[3] The binding launched the stage during which the penitent was excommunicated, that is, excluded from the eucharistic assembly, from church and sacrament. This period, lasting months to even years, comprised prayer, fasting, almsgiving, and symbolic gestures performed by the penitent with, notably, the pastor (bishop or priest) and even community members joining in some of those as well. The loosing occurred in the final stage, when the pastor readmitted the penitent to the liturgical assembly and allowed sharing in Holy Communion.[4]

Who were subject to such penitence? Those who's publicly known sins were so harmful to others and the commonweal as to scandalize and demoralize the church in its members, with the potential of tempting them to similar behaviors or at least indifference toward their occurrences. They numbered three: apostasy (sometimes called idolatry, since renouncing Christianity entailed performing Roman ritual sacrifices), adultery (in some places, expanded to notorious fornication), and murder (in some places, homicide).

The keys to learning from this ancient ritual process of *exomologesis*, which in its own time was not without significant problems, are what I would call its proper, pastoral humility and essentially

---

[3]   See John Mahoney, *The Making of Moral Theology: A Study of the Roman Catholic Tradition* (Oxford: Clarendon Press, 1987), 2–5.

[4]   See Bruce T. Morrill, *Practical Sacramental Theology: At the Intersection of Liturgy and Ethics* (Eugene, OR: Cascade Books, 2021), 59–60.

communal-social dimension. In its formality, *exomologesis* demonstrates the ecclesial impulse not to identify Christ's empowering of
his disciples to bind people to their sins with the eternal fate of
their souls, but rather with a pastoral duty to minister both mercy
and justice to the grave sinner and communal body, the church
and society going forward in this world. The church's received role
is a humble one, striving for the salvation of every person, while
knowing its proper place, namely, that it does not arbitrate from
the divine seat of final judgment. The rationale and concrete practices entailed in the process of *exomologesis*, I am proposing, invite
contemporary Catholic reflection on ways to practice penance and
reconciliation for the benefit of grave sinners and those they've
seriously harmed as well as the body of the church and the wider
society (the world) in which its institutions and all its members are
responsibly to participate. Space limitations allow me to offer just
two concluding points.

The first concerns the theology and practice of the sacrament
of penance ("going to confession") that succeeded *exomologesis* in
Western medieval Christianity was formalized by the sixteenth
century Council of Trent, and to this day functions in Roman
Catholicism as "the primary way of obtaining forgiveness and the
remission of serious sin committed after baptism."[5] The Second
Vatican Council's mandate for the restoration and renewal of this
sacrament has yet to be broadly realized in effective practice of
the Rite of Penance (1973), such that "going to confession" itself
often bears a certain scandalous reputation. Bernauer quotes as "a
very traditional Catholic view" that of the prominent Fr. Theodore
Hesburgh. Hesburgh describes his ministry in the confessional (the

---

[5]   John Paul II, "Reconciliation and Penance," Post-synodal Apostolic
Exhortation (December 2, 1984), no. 31, quoted in Bruce T. Morrill, "Sign of
Reconciliation and Conversion? Differing Views of Power—Ecclesial, Sacramental, Anthropological—Among Hierarchy and Laity," *Theological Studies*
75, no. 3 (2014), 598.

late-medieval-era partitioned booth that Catholics mostly prefer for celebrating the sacrament) as instinctually and professionally a matter of forgiveness of "everyone who comes in, confesses, and is sorry." The seeming instinct on Lohn's part to forgive Höss troubles Bernauer, but I am further troubled by Hesburgh's all too representative, popular explanation of the sacrament. Hesburgh presents it as a matter of an individual's request ("comes in"), confession, and expression of contrition ("is sorry"). This understanding has lent itself to notions of "cheap grace" with Protestants and many Catholics, having derided the sacrament as giving believers free license to do any sinful actions whatever with impunity, knowing they can get them forgiven cost free next Saturday in the confessional.

The actual, official Catholic tradition, in contrast to this "very traditional Catholic view," outlines the steps for the celebration of penance—contrition, confession, penance, and absolution—with precise specifications.[6] Drawing on decrees reaching back to Trent and the Code of Canon Law, the rite's introduction asserts that sincere contrition entails resolute intention, with the help of God's grace, not to persist in the sins confessed. The penitent may not be selective about the sins to be confessed, but rather is bound, after having carefully examined one's conscience, to confess all grave sins of which one is aware since one's last confession. Willfully withholding any nullifies the entire process, making the priest's ministration of absolution invalid. As for the penance (technically, the act of satisfaction or expiation) to be performed, the priest-confessor, making a "spiritual judgment," should tailor it to nature of the grave sin confessed, while ascertaining that the penitent agrees to being able to carry it out.[7] Indeed, at the beginning

---

[6]   See Rite of Penance (1973), nos. 6–7, in *Rites of the Catholic Church: Volume One* (Collegeville, MN: Liturgical Press, 1990), 528–31.

[7]   Notable to Bernauer's concern, the priest's "spiritual judgment," from Trent through the current rite, includes "his decision of forgiveness or retention of sins in accord with the power of the keys." See ibid., no. 4b.

of the ritual, the confessor is to ask about the penitent's state in life, if unknown to him. This is a far cry from the caricature of the sacrament as simply a matter of naming some sins and being dismissed to "say an Our Father, Hail Mary, and Glory Be." Still, the fact that the rite concludes with the priest giving the formal absolution, before the penitent actually does the act of penance/ satisfaction, leaves the sacrament susceptible to the kind of characterization that reduces the process simply to showing up, naming your sins, and saying you're sorry. The crucial corporate (ecclesial and social) dimension of the sacrament, which instruction on the overall renewed rite underlines,[8] the ritual procedure of confession often undermines.

My second point is to encourage continued evolution in the church's penitential tradition.[9] Catholics worldwide have since the late 1960s overwhelmingly abandoned the rite of confession,[10] with analysts finding people would prefer general, communal penitential rituals. To my mind, however, that leaves the acutely scandalous cases, such as Höss, insufficiently addressed for the sake of both the Christian faith's integrity and the church's mission in service to the modern world. While papal statements and symbolic gestures on behalf of the entire church in contrition for grave sins committed against peoples in the past became a hallmark of John Paul II (continued by Francis), there still need to be ways for the

---

[8] Ibid., no. 5. See also John Paul II, "Reconciliation," nos. 4, 8, 13, 16.

[9] In this I join fellow theologians specializing in this sacrament. See, among others, Monika K. Hellwig, *Sign of Reconciliation and Conversion: The Sacrament of Penance for Our Times* (Collegeville, MN: Liturgical Press, 1991); Jonathan Stotts, "Calling Down God's Mercy on the Body: Revisiting the Rite of General Confession and Absolution," *Liturgy: Journal of the Liturgical Conference* 34, no. 1 (2019), 39–47.

[10] Social-scientific studies within the past decade provide the statistics, while in 2002, Pope John Paul II described the practice of confession as in a state of crisis, reaching back to the 1970s. See Morrill, "Sign of Reconciliation and Conversion?," 601–604; Morrill, *Practical Sacramental Theology*, 73–75.

church, clergy, and laity to foster public repentance with believers who have gravely sinned and join them in periods of prayer, fasting, almsgiving, etc. The varied, complicated challenges are many, and ours certainly are different times from those of the ancient church. Still, taking responsibility with, perhaps in some measure even for, baptized members of the body of Christ in ways that express contrition and even make expiation toward the harmed (as possible) is arguably inherent to the practice of baptizing people in response to the scandalous gospel message of boundless divine mercy in the first place. The necessity of meeting the challenge becomes all the more evident by the fact that, unlike in 1947, the Roman Catholic Church now unequivocally condemns capital punishment and is committed to the abolition of the death penalty worldwide.[11]

---

[11] See Pope Francis, *Fratelli Tutti: Encyclical Letter on Fraternity and Social Friendship* (October 3, 2020), no. 263. See also *Catechism of the Catholic Church*, no. 2267, revised by Pope Francis.

16

An Auschwitz Absolution—
A Moral Scandal

Stanislaw Obirek

The invitation to write a short essay for this book is an honor for me, but also a difficult challenge. I undertake it only because the topic of absolution seems to me to be extremely important not only for religious but also for cultural reasons. Two books by Bernauer, which situate the problem of the absolution of the Commandant of Auschwitz by a Polish Jesuit in the broader context of the relationship between the Jesuits and Jews, are an important supplement to the topic; I have in mind a book coauthored with Robert Maryks in 2014, devoted to the meetings of Jesuits with Jews over the centuries,[1] and also Bernauer's reflection on the Jesuits and their attitude to the Holocaust and the Jews in 2019.[2] In both books, I find an honest and reliable confrontation with the complex past of the Jesuit Order, in which anti-Semitism was also present.

---

[1] James Bernauer and Robert A. Maryks, *"The Tragic Couple": Encounters between Jews and Jesuits* (Leiden, Germany: Brill, 2014).

[2] James Bernauer, *Jesuit Kaddish: Jesuits, Jews, and Holocaust Remembrance* (Notre Dame, IN: University of Notre Dame Press, 2019).

I have been dealing with the issues of the Holocaust for at least forty years, mainly in dialogue with Polish scholars. I have an impression that as a society we are unable to deal with this topic in an appropriate way. There are many reasons for this, but the most important are two: on the one hand, historical memory is politicized by the right-wing and populist governments; and on the other, the reluctance of the Catholic Church to face its own tradition of anti-Semitism. This first problem has been highlighted by Jan Grabowski,[3] one of the most distinguished researchers on the history of the Holocaust in Poland, and the second is by Jacek Leociak, one of the best experts in the history of the Warsaw ghetto in Poland.[4] There is no indication that this situation will change soon. Therefore, the proposal to reflect on the meaning of the absolution of Höss seems to be a good opportunity to reflect on the Catholic attitude toward the Holocaust of European Jews in general.

The topic of absolution of Auschwitz evokes in me not only mixed feelings. I consider the mere fact of absolving a war criminal a scandal. Perhaps if I had been in Lohn's shoes I would have acted the same. I do not mean to evaluate this gesture of absolution by a Catholic priest who did it with full conviction and in accordance with the doctrine of the Catholic Church. I am talking about the civilizational consequences of this gesture, which invalidates the metaphysical guilt that Karl Jaspers wrote about in The *Question of German Guilt*, based on lectures from 1945 to 1946.[5] Here a

---

[3]   Jan Grabowski, "Leaked Emails Show How the Polish Government Tried to Rewrite Holocaust History," *GW*, November 8, 2022, https://wyborcza.pl/7,173236,28781144,leaked-emails-show-how-the-polish-government-tried-to-rewrite.html - S.from_poland-K.P-B.1-L.2.zw.

[4]   Jacek Leociak, *Młyny boże. Zapiski o Kościele i Zagładzie* (Wołowiec, Poland: Wydawnictwo Czarne, 2018).

[5]   Karl Jaspers, *Question of German Guilt* (New York: Fordham University Press, 2000).

representative of the institution states that in the eyes of God, a criminal with millions of victims on his conscience and regretting his sins is not only acquitted but also assured to gain eternal happiness. For me, it is contrary to the elementary sense of justice. This is even more astonishing considering Höss's "confession" in which it is clear that his attitude toward Jews did not change at all.

My indignation has to do not only with Höss's absolution but with the Catholic Church's reaction to the drama of the Holocaust and especially with the open protection of war criminals after World War II. This practice has been documented quite well, and the Vatican itself has never referred to it, let alone condemned the priests and bishops involved in it. My opinion is supported by the film, *The Devil's Confession. Eichmann's Lost Tapes* (2022), based on conversations between Nazi criminals,[6] and by two books that are closely related to this film: one by Argentine journalist Uki Goni[7] and the other by German philosopher Bettina Stangneth.[8] Also, let me mention the figure of the little-known Jesuit Franciszek Ilków-Gołąb (1909–78), who was expelled from the Jesuits in 1949, probably because he refused to give absolution for crimes against Jews. Władysław Lohn, the confessor of Rudolf Höss, was his provincial during the war. This story was described by Fr. Michał Czajkowski who was a student of Ilków-Gołąb at the seminary in Wroclaw[9] in 2017.

The Devil's Confession is based on seventy-hour conversations in Argentina in the late 1950s with Adolf Eichmann, conducted

---

[6]   https://docaviv.co.il/2022-en/films/the-devils-confession-the-lost-eichmann-tapes/.

[7]   Uki Goni, *The Real Odessa: Smuggling the Nazis to Peron's Argentina* (London: Granta Books, 2002).

[8]   Bettina Stangneth, *Eichmann before Jerusalem* (New York: Alfred A. Knopf, 2014).

[9]   Michał Czajkowski, „Jezuita czasu wojny," in Zagłada Żydów, *Studia i Materiały*, no. 13 (2017), 759.

by Dutch journalist (also a Nazi criminal) Willem Sassen. At the end of these conversations, Eichmann says, "[I]f of the 10.3 million Jews … we had killed 10.3 million, I would be satisfied, and would say, good, we have destroyed an enemy."[10] Eichmann had in mind all European Jews. Sassen wrote down Eichmann's words in detail and submitted them to him for correction. The preserved record shows handwritten notes by Eichmann, who wanted these conversations to be used only for research purposes and published after his death. After Eichmann was captured by Israeli agents on May 11, 1960, and brought to Israel, Sassen sold the story to the American magazine *Life*. Already after the trial had begun, a seven-hundred–page transcript of these conversations was handed over to the Israeli prosecutor's office, which used some of them in the trial. When Eichmann claimed during the trial that he was just a small cog, Israeli attorney general Gideon Hausner confronted him with the records. Eichmann insisted they were quotes out of context.

Now I will say a few words about two books mentioned above. Uki Goni, Argentine investigative journalist, author of *True Odessa: As Peron Brought Nazi Criminals to Argentina*, writes that the main impetus for his writing was the overwhelming awareness of the falsification of the recent history of the country. According to his findings, Juan Peron, the Argentine army general who became president of that country, played a major role in the escape of Nazi criminals to Argentina. But it is also clear that a primary role was played by Catholic clergy. There were two cardinals—Eugene Tisserant, a Frenchman, and Antonio Caggiano, an Argentinean—and two bishops: Alois Hudal, an Austrian, and Augustin Barrere, an Argentinean. There were also several priests of various nationalities who actively participated in Nazi crimes. The cardinals worked closely with Pope Pius XII. Five of the greatest Nazi criminals were rescued by these various clergy: Erich Priebke, Gerhard Bohene,

---

[10]   Stangneth, *Eichmann before Jerusalem*, 293.

Josef Schwammberger, Josef Mengele, and Adolf Eichmann. A meeting of the cardinals in 1946 in Rome was of key importance, where a detailed plan was developed to "rescue" as many war criminals as possible. About Eichmann, Cardinal Caggiani said, "Our obligation as Christians is to forgive him for what he's done."[11] And so the theme of the criminal's absolution returns.

In *Eichmann before Jerusalem: The Unexamined Life of a Mass Murderer*, Bettina Stangneth raises questions of why we remain silent when we see evil happening and observe the criminals who commit it, and also why we succumb to lies. She gives a convincing answer: "The German people were only too happy to pretend that Eichmann had murdered six million Jews by himself."[12]

Finally, I return to the Jesuit Franciszek Ilków-Gołąb. We know the basic facts of his life,[13] but we know little about the reasons for his departure from the Jesuits. What we know is quite coincidental. Perhaps his correspondence with his provincial has been preserved in the Jesuit archives. Getting to know it would shed a lot of light on the key problem in the case of this "Auschwitz Absolution." The supposition that he was expelled from the Jesuit Order because he refused to grant absolution to murderers of Jews seems plausible. He was a lecturer in Stara Wieś from 1941 to 1943 (a village under German occupation in East Poland), and from 1943 to 1945 an ordinary priest in Lviv, which means that he was released from lecturing during the war. We know from his later life that he was a respected lecturer in several seminaries in Poland (Kielce, Kraków, Wroclaw, Nysa). He was well prepared for them thanks to his studies in Innsbruck, Rome, and a 1939

---

[11]   Goni, *The Real Odessa*, 317.

[12]   Stangneth, *Eichmann before Jerusalem*, 360.

[13]   Franciszek Ilków-Gołąb, *Encyklopedia wiedzy o jezuitach na ziemiach Polski i Litwy 1564–1995*, ed. L. Grzebień (Krakow, Poland: WAM Publishing, 1996), 227.

doctorate in theology earned in Vienna. Why was such a promising lecturer released from the Order? If the reason was, as suggested by Czajkowski (suggestion based on the opinion of the Jesuit Stanisław Szymański, a seminarian in Stara Wieś during the war),[14] then we have to think about the possibility that it was his rejection of absolution for war criminals. I am convinced that the explanation of this matter will shed light on the problem of absolution and the secret of confession in general.

---

[14]   Stansław Szymański, *Encyklopedia wiedzy o jezuitach na ziemiach Polski i Litwy 1564–1995*, ed. L. Grzebień (Krakow, Poland: WAM Publishing, 1996), 671.

CHRONOLOGY OF WŁADYSŁAW LOHN, SJ

April 5, 1889	Born in Gorzków.
June 18, 1904	Joins the Jesuits.
June 17, 1917	Ordained a priest.
1919–1921	Studies at the Gregorian University in Rome where he obtains a doctorate in theology.
1922–1928	Teaches theology in Krakow.
1928–1934	Lecturer on dogmatic theology in Gregorian University (Rome).
October 10, 1935	Appointed Jesuit provincial of southern Poland.
1940	Enters Auschwitz to plead for the release of Jesuits from his community who had been arrested. Meets Höss who refuses his plea but allows him to leave.
1946	Attends 29th General Congregation of the Jesuits (Rome, September 6 to October 23).
February 2, 1947	Retires as provincial.
April 10, 1947	Meets with the imprisoned Höss at the request of Cardinal Sapiecha (Archbishop of Krakow). The meeting lasts over four hours, and it includes hearing Höss's confession.
April 11, 1947	Returns to the prison and gives Höss communion.

April 12, 1947   Speaks in confidence to his Jesuit community about the meeting with Höss.

1947–1956   Works at and directs the publishing house of the Apostolate of Prayer.

1958   At the first mass of the just ordained Jesuit priest Władysław Kubik, recalls his encounter with Höss as an example of the demands of the priestly vocation of reconciliation. This is the year that Karol Wojtyla (later Pope John Paul II) is consecrated a bishop and appointed the Auxiliary Bishop of Krakow.

December 3, 1961   Dies in Krakow.

CHRONOLOGY OF RUDOLF HÖSS

November 25, 1900	Born in Baden-Baden.
1922	Enters the Nazi Party.
1923	Sentenced to a ten-year prison term for participating in a right-wing murder (he is pardoned in 1928).
1934–1938	Becomes a member of the SS and is on the staff of Dachau.
May 1940– December, 1943	Commandant of Auschwitz.
December 1, 1943	Moves to Berlin, named administrator of Economic-Administrative Office.
June, 1944	Returns to Auschwitz to preside over the murder of Hungarian Jews (initiative named Aktion Höss).
March 11, 1946	Höss, disguised as a farm laborer, arrested by the British.
April 2, 1947	Sentenced to death by Poland's Supreme National Tribunal.
April 4, 1947	Requests to see a priest.
April 7, 1947	Repeats in writing his request to see a priest.

April 10, 1947	Visited by Fr. Władysław Lohn, SJ, who hears his confession.
April 11, 1947	Receives communion from Lohn in prison.
April 11, 1947	Writes last letters to his wife and children.
April 12, 1947	Makes a declaration of guilt.
April 16, 1947	Executed in the Auschwitz camp, Fr. Tadeusz Zaremba at his side, reciting prayers for the dying.

Rudolf Höss:
Final Declaration[1]

April 12, 1947

"My conscience forces me to make the following declaration: In the seclusion of my detainment I arrived at the bitter knowledge of how enormous my crime against humanity has been. As commander of the Auschwitz extermination camp I executed part of the horrible human extermination plans of the 'Third Reich.' Thereby I caused the greatest harm against humanity and human solidarity. In particular, I caused the incredible suffering to the Polish people. I am atoning for my responsibility with my life. May God forgive me my actions one day. I ask for pardon from the Polish nation. In the Polish prisons I first experienced what human compassion [humanity, *Menschlichkeit*] means. In spite of all that happened I was shown a human compassion that I never expected and which shamed me profoundly. May the revelations and descriptions of the enormous crimes against humanity lead to the fact that in the future all prerequisites for such atrocious events will be prevented in advance!"

---

[1]   Archive of the Auschwitz-Birkenau State Museum, APMA-B, IZ-22/2, p. 5, cited in Manfred Deselaers, *And Your Conscience Never Haunted You?: The Life of Rudolf Höss, Commander of Auschwitz* (Auschwitz, Germany: Auschwitz-Birkenau State Museum, 2013), 224.

Acknowledgments

It is with pride and pleasure that I express my gratitude to some of those responsible for creating this volume. First of all, my deepest debt is to those who contributed essays. They responded with immediate interest and generosity to the invitation to participate. For suggesting certain scholars as potential contributors, thanks are owed to Professors Deborah Dwork and Robert Burns and to Dr. Joanna Silwa. Ms. Rachel Twombly, of the permissions office of Rowman and Littlefield, was helpful in securing the rights to the Höss memoir. Professor emeritus Alec Peck, president of the Boston College Association of Retired Faculty, encouraged the successful submission of an application for a retired faculty grant to cover the expense of securing the rights to the memoir. Scott Molony, the technical support person in the Jesuit community at Boston College, was skillful in his suggestions. Appreciation is due to Fr. Manfred Deselaers who works at the Center for Dialogue and Prayer at Auschwitz and who casually mentioned over lunch with James Bernauer that a Jesuit priest had heard the confession of Höss. That was the beginning of this volume's examination. Thanks are owed to Frs. Władysław Kubik, SJ, and Damian Mazur- kiewicz, SJ, whose memory and Jesuit archives provided some basic information regarding Fr. Lohn and his meeting with Höss. The book's editor at Orbis Books, Jon M. Sweeney, was enthusiastic and supportive about this project from the moment he saw our proposal. He also suggested the title of our book.